Coralations

Forerunners: Ideas First

Short books of thought-in-process scholarship, where intense analysis, questioning, and speculation take the lead

FROM THE UNIVERSITY OF MINNESOTA PRESS

(Continued on page 79)

Coralations

Melody Jue

University of Minnesota Press

MINNEAPOLIS
LONDON

Excerpts from Craig Santos Perez, "Sonnet at the Edge of the Reef," from *Habitat Threshold* (Omnidawn Publishing, 2020) published by permission of the poet. Portions of chapter 4 were previously published in a different form in "Submerging Inscription," in "Inscriptive Studies," ed. Paul Benzon and Rita Raley, special issue, *ASAP Journal* 7, no. 2 (May 2022); copyright 2022 Johns Hopkins University Press.

ISBN 978-1-5179-1812-5 (PB)
ISBN 978-1-4529-7193-3 (Ebook)
ISBN 978-1-4529-7288-6 (Manifold)

Published by the University of Minnesota Press, 2025
111 Third Avenue South, Suite 290
Minneapolis, MN 55401–2520
www.upress.umn.edu

Available as a Manifold edition at manifold.umn.edu

The University of Minnesota is an equal-opportunity educator and employer.

For Aurelia

Contents

Prologue. PANTONE 16–1546: Living Coral

"PANTONE 16–1546 LIVING CORAL" is an orangish-pink hue that was chosen as Pantone's Color of the Year in 2019 (Figure 1). Pantone describes "Living Coral" as "vivifying and effervescent" and "evocative of how coral reefs provide shelter to a diverse kaleidoscope of color."[1] Like many popularizations, this description portrays coral as a rainbow signifier of tropical marine life. Yet there is a magic trick here, a subtle act of substitution: Pantone writes that coral reefs shelter *color* instead of fish or other reef lifeforms. As a company that "provides a universal language of color" for use in industry and design, it is not surprising to see Pantone mobilize an ecological metaphor to talk about a diversity of color, as if colors themselves were lifeforms to be conserved.

"Living Coral" is a metonym on two levels: a color that stands in for a rainbow of other colors, and an iconic coral that stands in for a multiplicity of other corals. Metonymy, the act of referring to something via one of its attributes or parts, is about substitution: for example, invoking "the stage" to indicate the theater. "Living Coral" is not only metonymic but also a type of

1. Pantone, "Color of the Year," https://www.pantone.com/articles/color-of-the-year/color-of-the-year-2019.

xi

Figure 1. Pantone 16–1546: Living Coral.

a "global icon," a genre of sign that Bishnupriya Ghosh reminds us "always opens to an elsewhere" in a manner analogous to a camera aperture.[2] In Ghosh's camera analogy, a change in aperture results in a change in projected image. Similarly, a change in coral species or geography may lead to a completely different kind of story about coral than those that follow from stony, tropical, and colorful reefs. "Living Coral" thus offers an occasion to consider the deeper effects of a homogenous conception of coral and its implications for environmental narratives, scientific knowledge, and mediation.

Although "Living Coral" masquerades as a global icon for all corals, it references a very particular coral—*Corallium rubrum,*

2. Bishnupriya Ghosh, *Global Icons: Apertures to the Popular* (Durham, N.C.: Duke University Press, 2011), 9.

or red coral, which has been harvested from the Mediterranean since antiquity and valued as a type of gemstone. In Greek mythology, coral was thought to originate from the blood of the decapitated Medusa's head, dripping into the ocean, which hardened into red coral.[3] Sometimes referred to as "red gold," *Corallium rubrum* ranges from pale pink to dark red, and is in danger of disappearing from the Mediterranean due to overharvesting, habitat destruction, and climate change.[4] What is commonly understood as the universal color "coral," then, is indexed to *Corallium rubrum* rather than, say, violet coral, Hawaiian black coral, brown staghorn coral, multihued carnation coral, orange-tipped bubble coral, or coral fluorescence.[5]

At a time when corals around the world face a number of anthropogenic threats, it feels perverse that Pantone imagines "Living Coral" providing "comfort and buoyancy in our continually shifting environment."[6] The "shifting" environment is an understatement haunted by what it does not say—that corals are losing their ecological conditions of livability. As I write this in 2023, the world's oceans have experienced one of the hottest summers in living record. The global average daily sea surface temperature reached 20.96 Celsius, and sea temperatures in

3. Malcolm Shick, *Where Corals Lie: A Natural and Cultural History* (Chicago: University of Chicago Press, 2018).

4. Autumn Spann, "The Mediterranean's Red Coral Is Running Out," https://www.theatlantic.com/science/archive/2021/02/red-coral -mediterranean-fishing-climate-change/618124/.

5. For example, Or Ben-Zvi, Yoav Lindemann, Gal Eyal, and Yossi Loya, "Coral Fluorescence: A Prey-Lure in Deep Habitats," *Communication Biology* 5, no. 537 (2022), https://doi.org/10.1038/s42003 -022-03460-3.

6. Pantone, "Pantone Announces the Color of the Year 2019: PANTONE® 16–1546 Living Coral," https://www.pantone.com/articles /press-releases/pantone-announces-the-color-of-the-year-2019 -pantone-16-1546-living-coral.

places like the Florida coast reached over 100 Fahrenheit.[7] It is no surprise, then, that the reception of Pantone's "Living Coral" has been mixed; as journalist Christina Cauterucci writes, it "feels like a troll directed at a planet rapidly growing inhospitable to the many organisms that call it home."[8] "Living Coral" belies two kinds of dead coral: the gemstone commodity, and the reefs lost to multiple types of environmental degradation: ocean warming, coral bleaching, the pressures of ocean acidification, damage from climate-intensified storms, and other slow violences of anthropogenic climate change.[9]

These necropolitical contexts have motivated some to imagine a broader Pantone coral palette. Pantone partnered with the campaign "Glowing Glowing GONE" to recognize three new colors that correlate with tropical coral fluorescence, a biological phenomenon that occurs just before they bleach white from thermal stress. "Glowing Glowing GONE" markets three new shades, "Glowing Blue," "Glowing Yellow," and "Glowing Purple" as environmentally-conscious colors. Yet the campaign jarringly uses fluorescence to produce two different affects: the pathos of anticipating coral death, and the joy of using these colors to

7. "Ocean Surface Hits Highest Ever Recorded Temperature and Set to Rise Further," *The Guardian*, August 4, 2023, https://www.theguardian.com/environment/2023/aug/04/oceans-hit-highest-ever-recorded-temperature; "101°F in the Ocean off Florida: Was It a World Record?," *The New York Times*, July 26, 2023, https://www.nytimes.com/2023/07/26/climate/florida-100-degree-water.html.

8. Christina Cauterucci, "The 2019 Color of the Year Is the Latest Hilarious Misfire in Pantone's History of Awkward Wokeness Attempts," https://slate.com/human-interest/2018/12/pantone-color-of-the-year-2019-living-coral-climate-change.html.

9. Rob Nixon, *Slow Violence and the Environmentalism of the Poor* (Cambridge, Mass.: Harvard, 2011).

"design glowing products" and "create glowing events," as if the end of the world, for corals, is a rave.[10]

Still, "Glowing Glowing GONE" usefully destabilizes the correlation of coral with just one iconic color. I see the iconicity of "Living Coral" as a problem because attention in the sciences, humanities, and global environmentalisms has almost exclusively focused on one kind of coral, and one kind of environment: stony corals in warm, tropical waters. This occludes a number of exceptions. Not all corals build reefs: soft corals live in warms waters come in all kinds of pastels. Cold-water corals do not have symbiotic algae (are azooxanthellate) because they live mainly in cold, deep, and/or dark waters, and thus lack the pigments brought by algal companions. *Lophelia pertusa* is ghostly white—or ceramic white, or milky white. Fire corals are stinging to the touch, further away in the coral family tree from those stony corals that have become so iconic. Joining them are whip corals, mushroom-shaped purple sea pansies, sea pens, and other octocorals that build life worlds far different from tropical stony corals.

There is Living Coral (PANTONE 16–1546), and a multiplicity of other corals—corals that inhabit different ecologies, have different relations to extractive industries, enable different possibilities of world-building, and disrupt an environmental media imaginary calibrated to tropical waters and inscriptive archives.

10. "Glowing, Glowing, Gone," https://www.glowing.org/show
-your-colours-challenge.

'

Introduction: Coralations

LIVING CORAL is the iconic surface underneath which we must dive. I have intentionally chosen Pantone's "Living Coral" for the cover of this small book in order to explore the question of what exceeds, or deviates from, the common imaginary of corals. Within the volumetric space between the book's coralline covers, I draw attention to the inadequacy of any one color for addressing the range of variation in actual corals, unfolding the ways that artists and scholars have used corals to rethink relations with gender, empire, and media.

Coralations is a philosophical exploration of the many corals that do not conform to the iconicity of Coral.[1] When we think of Coral with a capital C—and I use "we" to indicate a broad public that reads and produces discourse about global corals—what comes to mind is something like this: a stony, branching organism that lives in warm, balmy waters. Coral alternates between signifying an organism and signifying an environment, all too often imagined as a tourist destination, tropically distributed. In *Coral Empire: Underwater Oceans, Colonial Tropics, and Visual Modernity* (2019), Ann Elias cau-

1. I capitalize *Coral* when it refers to the broad public imagination of corals.

Figure 2. Hovering over corals in Fiji. Photograph by Melody Jue, 2020.

tions that even in the early twentieth century, "Photographers and cinematographers saw an opportunity to generate on film a coral orientalism," treating coral as a colorful and exotic other to promote a homogenous view of the tropics.[2] Troubling the boundaries between animal, vegetable, and mineral, corals are scientifically described as colonial organisms, colonies of tiny polyps that slowly build calcium carbonate skeletons and live

2. Ann Elias, *Coral Empire: Underwater Oceans, Colonial Tropics, Visual Modernity* (Durham, N.C.: Duke University Press, 2019), 21.

symbiotically with pigment-giving algae. Corals are also icons of precarity: they are in danger of bleaching when ocean waters become too warm, causing them to eject their symbiotic algae and turn bone white. A photograph of bleached-white coral is, to use a term from Roland Barthes, a type of denoted or "non-coded iconic" image—an image easy to mistake as purely literal (or "naïve"), even as it emits all kinds of learned significations.[3] Where Barthes famously analyzed the effect of "Italianicity" in a Panzani pasta ad, the bleached-white images of coral suggest mournability, drawn from the viewer's external knowledge of climate change and the repeated exposure to images of corals dying—a narrative that Irus Braverman focuses on in *The Coral Whisperers: Scientists on the Brink* (2019), tracking the way coral scientists negotiate feelings of hope and despair.

If Coral usually implies rainbow-hued reefs bathed in a warm-water environment with plenty of sunlight, what about the massive reefs of bone-white *Lophelia pertusa* that exist off the coast of Norway and in cold, deep waters of the Gulf of Mexico? If Coral assumes stony reef-builders that build up over the life of the colony, then what about soft corals, whose fleshy hydroskeletons bloom and deflate with the changing of the tides? In the reflections that follow, I work through how an iconic sense of Coral lends itself to certain media analogies—to photography, to books—analogies that turn out to not be so universal when one pays attention to the life-worlds and milieu-specific relations of particular corals.

Environmental media is a capacious field of study: it includes media that represent the environment or environmentalist concerns, but also elements of the environment that perform analogous functions as anthropogenic forms of media, including the

3. Roland Barthes, "The Rhetoric of the Image," in *Image, Music, Text* (New York: Hill and Wang, 1977), 32–51.

transmission, storage, and processing of information.[4] What I mean by environmental media in this book includes elements of the environment that perform mediating effects—such as the role of seawater as a kind of photographic lens, filtering sunlight toward the upstretched tentacles of coral and their photosynthesizing algae.[5] The documentary *Chasing Coral* (2017), directed by Jeff Orlowski, anticipates and captures the process of a devastating coral bleaching event near New Caledonia but also examines some of the ways that corals are forms of archival media for the ocean climate. Just like terrestrial trees, stony corals also possess growth rings that accrete over a lifetime. In this way, stony corals slowly build up like stone books, mortared in place through the secretions of the living polyps. Yet as we will see, soft corals do not build such stratigraphic layers—their vibrantly colored bodies leave few traces when they die, as ephemeral as the petals of a flower. If not all corals are books, then how effective are conservation narratives that use the book as an analogy, taking disappearing reefs as akin to losing a library? How can we develop storytelling tactics that address the diversity and range of coral relations, when the protagonist does not just default to stony, reef-building corals?

The bias towards reef-building, or hermatypic, corals exists across both the sciences and humanities, shaping research questions, data sets, and narratives. In the sciences, attention to tropical corals is related to access and funding; it is much easier to study corals in shallow tropical waters than deep-water corals like *Lophelia pertusa,* which require expensive equipment (boat time, Remotely Operated Vehicles [ROVs], sonar technol-

---

4. Friedrich Kittler, *Dracula's Vermächtnis: Technische Schriften* (Liepzig, Germany: Reclam, 1993), 8.
5. Irus Braverman, *Coral Whisperers: Scientists on the Brink* (Los Angeles: University of California Press, 2018).

ogies) that is often easiest to acquire through cooperation with industries—particularly the oil industry, which already uses these technologies for prospecting. In addition, many scientific maps of the global distribution of coral center on warm-water corals completely, leaving out the geographic distribution of cold-water corals.[6] This has likely had an effect on the humanities: to the best of my knowledge, all of the book-length humanities studies of coral focus on tropical stony corals, with the one exception of Malcolm Shick's excellent visual history *Where Corals Lie* (2018)—though Shick himself is a retired coral biologist.[7]

In this book, the word *coralations* is a portmanteau that evokes coral correlations, and coral relations—those things or conditions that share a notable connection or interdependency with corals. The *Oxford English Dictionary* traces the use of the word *correlation* as the "mutual relation of two or more things" to the

6. Allen Coral Atlas, https://allencoralatlas.org/.

7. Coral books in the arts and humanities that focus on tropical, stony corals include Ann Elias, *Coral Empire* (2019); C. Ann Klaus, *Drawing the Sea Near* (Durham, N.C.: Duke University Press, 2020); Greg Dvorak, *Coral and Concrete: Remembering Kwajalein Atoll between Japan, America, and the Marshall Islands* (Honolulu: University of Hawai'i Press, 2018); Irus Braverman, *Coral Whisperers* (2018). There is one chapter in Peter Godfrey Smith's *Metazoa* that philosophically reflects on soft corals. In terms of article-length works, see *"Lophelia pertusa* Conservation in the North Sea Using Obsolete Offshore Structures as Artificial Reefs" by Paulina Bergemark and Dolly Jørgenson, *Marine Ecology Progress Series* 516 (December 3, 2014): 275–80. There is also some archaeological/historical research about cold-water corals: referencing Sophie Ann Adams's unpublished MA thesis, the authors of *Grave Goods* write, "cold water coral (*Lophelia pertusa*) washed up from the Atlantic waters around Scotland, represents the nearest source: she [Adams] cites the Roman author Ausonius, who described both the 'red corals and the white berries, fruit of the shell' found in these waters" (199), quoted in *Grave Goods: Objects and Death in Prehistoric Britain* by Anwen Cooper, Duncan Garrow, Catriona Gibson, Melanie Giles and Neil Wilkin (Oxford, UK: Oxbow, 2022).

sixteenth century, while the statistical sense of correlation as the "interdependence of two or more variable quantities such that a change in the value of one is associated with a change in the value or the expectation of the others" originates with eugenicist Francis Galton in the nineteenth century.[8] "Correlation's eugenicist history matters," media theorist Wendy Chun reminds us, "not because it predisposes all uses of correlation towards eugenics, but rather because when correlation works, it does so by making the present and future coincide with a highly curated past," enacting "a future that would repeat their discriminatory abstractions."[9] In her important study of big data industries, Chun evaluates how correlations become tied to *predictions,* a practice which risks reifying protected categories such as race, gender, and socioeconomic status. Taking Chun's precautions seriously, *Coralations* is not about applying an abstract theory of correlation *to* the study of corals, but about addressing the implications of correlating corals with the tropics, color, symbiosis, books as archival media, and photography—and how this impacts how we write about climate change.

"Coralation" is a pun that has independently occurred to many people. For example, the nonprofit organization CORALations, founded in 1995 by Mary Ann Lucking and Orlando Peraza, focuses on coral conservation in Puerto Rico and the wider Caribbean.[10] Similarly, artist Nicholas Magnan's 2022 film *Core Coralations* dwells with an archive of coral core samples at the Australian Institute of Marine Science's Coral Core facility and

8. See also Stephen M. Stigler, "Francis Galton's Account of the Invention of Correlation," *Statistical Science* 1, no. 2 (May 1989): 73–79.

9. Wendy Chun, *Discriminating Data: Correlation, Neighborhoods, and the New Politics of Recognition* (Cambridge, Mass.: MIT Press, 2022), 52.

10. CORALations, https://www.coralations.org/about_coralations/index.htm.

the specter of impending coral death.[11] The film visually plays with how scientists use UV lighting to detect correlations between coral growth bands and environmental changes.[12] In her evocative 2022 short essay, "Coralations: Returning to Breath," Irus Braverman imagines coralations as a way of thinking through the intimacies of corals as multispecies assemblages, co-saturating with law.[13] Braverman writes that the idea of "coralations" came to her "when contemplating the vibrant inter-relations among various coral parts as well as between corals and other living beings," and like Magnan, notes the important correlations between coral reefs and climate.[14] The aim of this book differs from Braverman's essay in its aspiration to not only *trace* dominant coralations (corals with tropicality, corals with records of the climate) but to think with corals that actively question and break normative coralations or stereotypes about Coral, building up pictures of other possible coralations to be addressed—for example, the coralation between *Lophelia pertusa* and sites of petroleum infrastructure and extraction (chapter 3).

In this book, my method is to follow a concept and explore how it offers a window—or, following Ghosh, an aperture—into the iconicity of Coral, centering moments in which such iconicity no longer holds. Sometimes this means following particular coral species, and sometimes this means examining how aesthetic engagements with corals lead us to question long-standing assumptions. To offer a brief sketch of the narrative to follow, *Coralations* begins by examining the dominant coralations of

11. Nicholas Mangan, "Core Coralations," https://suttongallery.com.au/exhibitions/core-coralations-death-assemblages/.

12. Nicholas Mangan, personal email, 2023.

13. Irus Braverman, "Coralations: Back to the Breath," *Queensland Review* 28, no. 2 (2022): 1–4.

14. Braverman, 2.

tropical stony corals (chapter 1, "Building"), then shifts to moments where they break down (chapter 2, "Softness"), examines how new coralations with petromodernity come into focus with cold-water corals (chapter 3, "Coldness"), traces how corals themselves have inspired ways of uncorrelating constructs like gender (chapter 4, "Grafting"), analyzes how corals have been the subjects of and models for algorithmic correlations (chapter 5, "Optimization"), and concludes with a close reading of Craig Santos Perez's "Sonnet by the Edge of a Reef" (Conclusion, "Edges"). These chapters interweave a range of media forms, including speculative fiction (Nalo Hopkinson, Ken Liu), documentary film (Jeff Orlowski, *Chasing Coral*), photography (Nadia Huggins), poetry (Craig Santos Perez), visual art (Christine and Margaret Wertheim, *Hyperbolic Crochet Coral Reef*; Ellen Gallagher, *Coral Cities*), and interactive media (NeMO-Net app). Such a range of media forms is necessary, as I will show, because of the ways that corals and media forms are reciprocally thought through each other. For example, while corals have been the objects of photography and photomosaic surveys, in *Coral Empire* Ann Elias traces how corals have been thought of, ontologically, as photosensitive media in the lens-like clarity of tropical waters; however, this media analogy does not hold for cold-water corals (chapter 3), which do not have symbiotic algae and live in deep, dark habitats. In another feedback loop, algorithms have been developed to process large photographic data sets of corals, while at the same time, corals have served as models for developing problem-solving algorithms (chapter 5).

The iconic imaginary of Coral is not something I want to entirely throw away; after all, it has been mobilized in environmentalist discourse to cultivate a widespread public care for the importance of coral reef environments, from their visual beauty to their importance as habitats and nurseries for all kinds of fish and other marine life. Coral can be a powerful icon, one of the few invertebrates to gather sustained public attention; and notably, Coral does this as an organism without a face. However, the iconic imaginary of Coral also standardizes, homogenizes, and normativizes a sense of corals. This narrows the kinds of stories we can tell, simplifies their relations, and forecloses a more capacious environmental media imaginary. My hope is that rethinking the limitations of Coral, through the mediations of particular corals in specific contexts of place, will lead to new, unexpected, and compelling environmental narratives that capture public attention—rather than reproduce a sense of despair upon hearing the same narratives of dying reef systems. Thinking past the iconicity of Coral is a kind of accounting that should lead to more expansive senses of environmental media, more inclusive goals for multispecies justice, and more nuanced forms of oceanic care work.

1. Building

STONY CORALS ARE BUILDERS OF WORLDS. In the chants of the Hawaiʻian Kumulipo, the first beings created out of the darkness were corals: "Hanau ka ʻUku-koʻakoʻa, hanau kana, he ʻAkoʻakoʻa, puka / Born was the coral polyp, born was the coral, came forth."[1] In the Marshall Islands, when Lowa (the uncreated) hummed, islands, reefs, and sandbanks emerged.[2] As anthropologist Greg Dvorak recounts in *Coral and Concrete: Remembering Kwajalein Atoll between Japan, America, and the Marshall Islands* (2018), the Ri-Kuwajleen, the Islanders who first settled Kwajelein, "understood in their oral traditions that the entire atoll, this whole ring of islets, originated from one massive coral head in the center of the lagoon, known as Tarlan."[3] In these origin stories, stony corals are the foundation of islands and life.

A different sense of corals as builders emerges in Western scientific contexts, placing corals more as the architects of created

1. Holumua Marine Initiative, "Coral Life Cycle," https://dlnr.hawaii.gov/holomua/coral-life-cycle/.

2. Pacific Islands Education Partnership, "Marshall Islands," http://pcep.prel.org/locations/marshall-islands/#:~:text=Marshall%20Islands%20Yokwe&text=In%20ancient%20times%2C%20when%20there,to%20constantly%20circle%20the%20sky.

3. Dvorak, *Coral and Concrete*, 19.

structures than as sacred origin points. Malcolm Shick notes how the Great Barrier Reef has been described as a "gigantic and irregular fortification, a steep glacis crowned with a broken parapet wall."[4] Shick dedicates a whole chapter to "Coral Construction" in *Where the Corals Lie* (2018), noting the ways that coral has been imagined as an architectural form as well as used as a stony resource (coral rock) to quarry and build temples, pyramids, and other structures. Such architectural language, as Stefan Helmreich notes, also appears in Darwin's many writings about corals and the formation of atolls. Take this quote from *Voyages of the Beagle*: "We feel surprise when travelers tell us of the vast dimensions of the Pyramids and other great ruins, but how utterly insignificant are the greatest of these, when compared to these mountains of stone accumulated by the agency of various minute and tender animals!"[5] Here, corals are lauded for exceeding even the pyramids in size and scale. Yet for Darwin, corals not only demonstrated a kind of agency as builders whose geologic structures that continue growing into the present; in his theory of atoll formation, he posited that corals gradually grew on top of extinct volcanoes that gradually subsided into the sea, leaving a coral ring that grew upwards near the ocean's surface.[6] In her classic 1983 literary study *Darwin's Plots*, Gillian Beer notes how Darwin's thoughts also drifted to coral when he diagrammed the tree of life: "the tree of life should perhaps be called the coral of life, base of branches dead; so that passages

4. Shick, *Where the Corals Lie,* 189.

5. Darwin's *Voyage of the Beagle* (1839), as cited in Stefan Helmreich, *Sounding the Limits of Life: Essays in the Anthropology of Biology and Beyond* (Princeton, N.J.: Princeton University Press, 2015), 50.

6. Haley Dunning, "Darwin's Coral Conundrum," https://www .nhm.ac.uk/discover/charles-darwin-coral-conundrum.html.

cannot be seen."[7] Unlike the tree of life, the figure of coral could account for the organisms that had already lived (the dead coral skeleton) to arrive at the living tips of the present—an ongoing architectural formation.

In a useful conceptual inversion, Helmreich suggests that we consider the way cultural representations of corals have accreted over time, and that perhaps such representations have *themselves* become discursive "scaffoldings upon which reefs have already been written."[8] What is valuable about this formulation is the reversal of the architectural metaphor. Discursive patterns (not just calcium carbonate) accrete over time, and representations and descriptions of coral reefs form into a structure upon which our understandings of coral are built. Drawing inspiration from Donna Haraway's likening of crafting conversation on common reading and writing to the process of reef building, Helmreich channels attention to how densely reefs "become prefigured through the historically layered descriptions of biologists, fisherpeople, ecologists, and, occasionally [. . .] anthropology."[9] Similarly, Dvorak writes that human beings are also "reef organisms" that bring their own histories to the reef, citing Edward Said's casual take on Antonio Gramsci's description of culture as "coral-like."[10] Knowing the tendencies through which corals have been figured is a first step in examining processes of coralation.

A key discursive scaffolding upon which coral has been figured is empire. In *Coral Empire* (2019), Ann Elias notes that at the end of the nineteenth century Great Britain not only owned most of

7. Gillian Beer, *Darwin's Plots: Evolutionary Narrative in Darwin, George Eliot, and Nineteenth-Century Fiction* (Oxford: Oxford University Press, 1983), 261n12.

8. Helmreich, *Sounding the Limits of Life,* 49.

9. Helmreich, 49.

10. Dvorak, *Coral and Concrete,* 22–23.

the world's coral empires but also chose to see in coral reefs a justification for their own imperial ambitions. Coral was seen to industriously build expansive reef structures, just as Great Britain built its empire:

> The imperial imaginary found in the figure of the coral reef a useful political image and a metaphorical space to assert the rightness and goodness of the empire's own colonizing practice of expansion. Acquiring and building colonies, especially in the tropics, seemed as organic for the British Empire as the process of reef building itself. And, in an age of positivist science and Enlightenment influence, a marine animal that also built toward the light embodied a useful social symbol for enlightened Europeans.[11]

Elias notes that this metaphor of coral as empire builder focused on the labor of white Europeans while obscuring other figurative reef builders—Indigenous laborers. Yet in a different vein, Elias cites a 1915 headline calling the acquisition of the Gilbert and Ellice Islands (now Kiribati and Tuvalu) "lumps of coral" part of a "vocabulary of domination" characterizing the people and culture of these islands as an "indiscriminate conglomerate."[12] Emphasizing the stoniness of coral in this instance framed coral as an object to be owned, rather than as a fellow empire-building organism to be emulated.

Elias's diagnosis of coral empire finds echoes in contemporary data visualizations of cities. In one example, geospatial specialist Craig Taylor manipulated European city transportation networks to evoke the patterns of branching corals. Taylor took flat road maps and gave them a slight three-dimensional lift, creating coral cities that seem to grow up and outward from a dense center. Selecting the most "livable" European cities,

11. Elias, *Coral Empire*, 18.
12. Elias, 19.

Taylor writes that he has been, "fascinated by the concept of making city networks look like living corals," coloring them in varied neons that evoke an undersea fantasy.[13] These are not the neons of Pantone's "Glowing Glowing Gone" campaign, which signal coral endangerment from climate change. The images are abstractions, where the environment disappears. Elements of each city's landscape can be inferred through blank spaces, suggesting "patterns where physical features such as rivers, oceans and mountains impact the network" of the city.[14] Further, what is invisible in these diagrams is the history of European colonialism, which extracted resources for the growth of these cities-as-corals from coral islands around the world.

Coral has also been part of empire building through its material use in colonialist architecture and transportation infrastructure. Across the Pacific, airport runways were created from dynamited and crushed up corals to form concrete. Dvorak notes that in the Marshall Islands, reef rocks were used to build "concrete seawalls, buildings, and the first airstrip."[15] In *Coral and Concrete,* Dvorak develops concrete as a telling historical metaphor:

> In contrast to the coralline model of history, which acknowledges the agency of individuals in terms of the larger reef, conventional histories usually teach about the victories and losses of nations. I refer in this book to these kinds of layers of history as "concrete." In Kwajelein and many other heavily militarized islands throughout Oceania, coral was literally used as an aggregate, mixed with cement and water to form quick-drying concrete that could be used to construct fortifications or to form roads

13. Craig Taylor, "Coral Cities: An Ito Design Lab Concept," https://towardsdatascience.com/coral-cities-an-ito-design-lab-concept-c01a3f4a2722.

14. Taylor.

15. Dvorak, *Coral and Concrete*, 26.

and runways. Concrete is the pulverization, amalgamation, and flattening of all these coralline histories into one condensed and monolithic mass.[16]

If Darwin's figuration of coral as a builder emphasized the glory of its enduring structures, Dvorak's metaphor of concrete draws attention to the destruction and pulverization of living coral reefs in the service of imperial and settler-colonial building projects. Concrete implies a different figure of temporality than strata: instead of being laid down one residue at a time (like a coral secreting its skeleton), the making of concrete involves the active destruction of corals in order to form new layers of pavement. The formation of one historical layer depends on the destruction of other historical layers—if one takes seriously coral skeletons as a kind of ecological record of the climate, akin to tree rings. Dvorak writes that concrete is "the actual physical process by which colonialism and militarism in the Pacific Islands have attempted to reduce the multiplicities of coral into something that is uniform, predictable, and homogenous" or that which "hegemonizes history."[17]

For anthropologist Cameron McKean, a closer consideration of coral strata offers another nonlinear figure of "melted temporality."[18] McKean recalls the history of how scientists came to read layers of calcium carbonate in the skeletons of corals for temporal significance, forming a kind of "mineral chronometer" or metric of time like tree rings. In his essay "Calcium Carbonate," McKean notes that our ability to translate "the coral's rhythmic carbonate growth into numerical clock time"

16. Dvorak, 25.

17. Dvorak, 26.

18. Cameron McKean, "Calcium Carbonate," https://culanth.org /fieldsights/calcium-carbonate.

originated from the work of three scientists who were studying the effects of radiation on reefs at Enewetak Atoll:

> They laid coral slices on light-sensitive paper, and after forty days, strontium-90 hidden in the skeleton unexpectedly materialized as glowing bands in the images, revealing an annual growth pattern that transformed the fragments into "coral chronometers." We can translate coral time today because humans—the U.S. military—drastically altered the matter inside the reefs of Enewetak Atoll. Coral time and human time melted together in the shadow of a mushroom cloud.[19]

The word *melted* is key. Rather than see the striated coral archives as the opposite of Dvorak's concrete—separated, rather than blended—McKean shows how coral archives tell time while also ontologically attesting to melted time. In the passage above, what McKean means by "coral time" includes "the moon-linked time of coral polyps, the seasonal oscillations of sea surface temperatures," temporalities that blur together with "jagged rhythms of technoscience" and the Anthropocene—which some geologists have found useful to date to the advent of the nuclear age, because it provides a "golden spike" in the global stratigraphic record. Yet McKean argues that the concept of a temporal rupture doesn't make sense in the case of calcium carbonate, "a mineral compound in which temporalities melt together."[20] Both McKean's figure of melting and Dvorak's figure of concrete examine the ways in which coral skeletons—sliced and sampled into scientific archives, or pulverized into the settler-colonial infrastructures of air transport—attest to registers of time in which the legacies of military destruction, settler colonialism, ocean

19. McKean.
20. McKean.

acidification, and the biological rhythms of corals themselves cannot be easily separated out from one another.[21]

However, to single out corals as the only builders or building material is to ignore a host of other multispecies agencies that contribute to reef formation. As Shick notes, "Other organisms of the reef community contribute to its three-dimensional structure. Some of these provide the calcareous debris of their own skeletons that forms sediments mortaring the interstices of the reef framework and strengthening it."[22] Reef-building algae are one notable force. Taiwan's Datan Algal Reef was named a "Hope Spot" by the ocean nonprofit organization Mission Blue, given its importance to ocean biodiversity and surprising size. Such algal reefs were just starting to be scientifically studied after World War II. American phycologist William Randolph Taylor was commissioned to visit the Marshall Islands and map their baseline algae just prior to the testing of atomic weapons and their ecological devastation. Taylor waxed poetic about the calcareous red algae *Porolithon,* which formed massive ridges on the windward side of Bikini Atoll and other islands, which he knew would be destroyed soon after his survey. One can read his 1950 book, *Plants of Bikini and Other Northern Marshall Islands,* as a kind of epitaph for algal reefs later annihilated by atomic testing.

21. As Marion Endt-Jones notes, it is this evidentiary sense of coral that contributes to its connection to another kind of building and institution, the zoological museum; for nineteenth-century naturalists like Ernst Haeckel, coral colonies not only appeared in museum dioramas but could each be thought of ontologically as "a small zoological museum." Quoted in Marion Endt-Jones, "A Monstrous Transformation: Coral in Art and Culture," in *Oceans,* ed. Pandora Syperek and Sarah Wade (London and Cambridge: Whitechapel Press with MIT Press, 2023), 108.

22. Shick, *Where Corals Lie*, 30.

Sometimes the presence of non-coral organisms indirectly contributes to reef formation by influencing the flow of seawater through "baffling." As Shick writes,

> Octocorals such as sea fans, sea whips and other alyconaceans baffle and slow the water currents moving across the reef. Crustose coralline red algae help to cement such sediments and larger fragments of coral rubble, cohering the composite. . . . Deep inside the reef, seawater chemistry and physics, and microbial activity, gradually transform the calcareous debris into sedimentary coral rock in the process of diagenesis.[23]

To baffle, here, means to slow a liquid flow. It is hard to resist that other sense of *baffle,* which means to astound or confuse. That the architectural forms of reef organisms "baffle" flows of water feels especially poetic to us terrestrial beings, who may have ignored something: while it is common to think of reefs as the media of inscription for records of the climate, here we have an example where water is a sculptural medium of inscription for the living form of a reef, whose shape influences three-dimensional contours of flow.

Baffling is complemented by bioerosion, as reef borers like mollusks and worms, urchins and fish, burrow and scrape away at reefs, contributing to the production of debris and sand. I am compelled to mention that while diving in Oahu in 2013, I observed the marks of "pencil urchins," echinoderms with thick spines. Their beaks had carved away at the volcanic rock in deep tracks, scraping away edible algae. I could not help but note the curious convergence of a media form (pencil) and an organism performing a kind of inscriptive work. Such marine organisms might be thought of as agents of mediation through their sculptural, inscriptive, and erosive work.

23. Shick, 30–31.

We can also find evidence of more-than-coral agencies at work in the skeletons of stony corals themselves. The authors of *Biology of Coral Reefs* (2009) note that "Microbial communities are not only associated with the coral surface and tissues, but with the coral skeleton too. About 98% of reef-building corals contain filamentous green algae, as well as cyanobacteria, fungi, and bacteria in their skeletons, where they form a series of distinct horizontal bands."[24] If, as Shick writes, a coral's "skeletal foundation represents the colony's history writ in stone and chemistry," this is a history that includes many microbial co-authors.[25] What Scott F. Gilbert elaborates as the coral "holobiont"—the organism plus its community of symbionts—is recorded in its skeleton.[26]

Coral skeletons are also histories of the minerality of seawater itself. Stony corals, after all, build their calcium carbonate skeletons from minerals they acquire in the surrounding ocean. To poetically convey this, Shick cites a stunning nineteenth-century metaphor: "the quarry from which they [corals] dug their masonry was the limpid wave."[27] Here, the liquid ocean is figured as a rock quarry, and seawater is the stone to be mined for building materials. To call the quarry *limpid*—clear, glassy, and unclouded—grates against the expected visual density of rock. It is an instance of the tendency to figure the oceanic in terms of the terrestrial, what I and others have elsewhere called a terres-

24. Charles R. C. Sheppard, Simon K. Davy, Graham M. Pilling, eds., *Biology of Coral Reefs* (Oxford: Oxford University Press, 2009), 123.

25. Shick, *Where Corals Lie*, 30.

26. Scott F. Gilbert, "Holobiont by Birth: Multilineage Individuals as the Concretion of Cooperative Processes," in *Arts for Living on a Damaged Planet*, ed. Anna Tsing, Heather Swanson, Elaine Gan, and Nils Bubandt (Minneapolis: Minnesota Press, 2017).

27. "Coral Rings," *Blackwood's Edinburgh Magazine* 74 (July–December 1853): 371. Quoted in Shick, *Where Corals Lie*.

trial bias at the level of language.[28] And yet, the image remains a striking reminder of the minerality of seawater. Consider a moment in N. K. Jemisin's Hugo Award–winning speculative fiction novel *The Fifth Season*: the main character, Essun, can control powerful geologic forces, but has difficulty with the "the strange slipperiness of seawater minerals."[29] Or, think of André Breton's description of stony corals in *Mad Love* (1937) as a "petrifying fountain," organisms that form hard bodies out of the liquidity of the ocean, much like the way limestone caverns form from droplets of water.[30] In the context of coral architectures, seawater sustains the fleshy bodies of coral polyps and multispecies marine life, the medium from which corals glean the minerals they need to survive and grow. Seawater is the environmental precondition for coral formation, a fact that is easy to forget once coral is taken out of the ocean to become building material.

To dwell with the minerality of seawater, I now turn to Nalo Hopkinson's short story "Repatriation" (2019). "Repatriation" first appeared in the online collection Current Futures, which, as literary scholar Elizabeth Deloughrey importantly notes, was sponsored by XPrize, which in turn is funded by the oil company Royal Dutch Shell.[31] While I agree with Deloughrey that Current Futures risks giving oil companies a social license to operate

28. Melody Jue, *Wild Blue Media: Thinking through Seawater* (Durham, N.C.: Duke University Press, 2020).

29. N. K. Jemisin, *The Fifth Season* (New York: Orbit, 2015), 384.

30. André Breton, *Mad Love,* trans. Mary Ann Caws (1937; New York: Bison Books, 1987), 10–12. This description comes on the heels of a passage exploring his fascination with crystals. I am grateful to an anonymous peer reviewer of the manuscript of this book for pointing me to Breton's image.

31. Elizabeth Deloughrey, "Mining the Seas: Speculative Fictions and Futures" in *Laws of the Sea: Interdisciplinary Currents* (Taylor and Francis, 2022), ed. Irus Braverman.

through the performance of environmental care, "Repatriation" nonetheless dramatizes the worldbuilding capacity of corals in a unique way. "Repatriation" follows Carleton and his husband Jerry just as they are about to embark on a surprise birthday cruise. Carleton is reluctant from the start, dwelling with the discomfort of taking a leisure cruise that evokes memories of dispossession from their hometown of Falmouth, Jamaica, which has since been swallowed by sea-level rise. At one point, Carlton grumbles,

> My husband had lost his goddamned mind. We both grew up as boys watching the cruise ships dock at our island, stinking up the port with the smell of tarry bunker fuel, disgorging tourists from foreign who would party for a few hours before jumping back on their travelling hotels for the next port of call. We would stare at them, our fingers clenched in the diamond-shaped holes of the chain link fencing that prevented us locals from accessing our own port unless we were working for the cruise line and could show papers to prove it.

Hopkinson offers a concise picture of capitalist and neocolonial dispossession, portraying the cruise ships as sea monsters that "disgorge" their tourists for temporary recreation while shutting out the locals, who are left clutching chain-link fencing through "diamond-shaped holes." If coastal access is a precious resource, then the chain-link fencing serves as a visual metaphor for that which has been extracted or taken away from local boys like Carlton and Jerry.

In face of further dispossession by sea level rise, corals become the agents of an unexpected kind of world-building. By the end of the story, Carlson finds that the ship is not a neocolonial discount cruise, but a repurposed architecture that is on its last voyage back to Falmouth, Jamaica, to help restore the climate-damaged harbor. Via the novum of biorock—an actual technique that scientists have experimented with—the capitalist architecture of cruise ships becomes a new sunken foundation for future coral growth and harbor restoration.[32] The biorock works by running a current through the steel frame of the ship to encourage calcification from the surrounding seawater, enabling the growth of corals and marine plants. Here, mineral-laden seawater and rock-forming corals work together as agents of environmental remediation, or even terraforming, growing atop the encrusted forms of cruise ships. After the metal ships sink like whale falls (suggested by the ship's name, *Cetacean of the Seas*), the corals transform what was an exploitative and capitalist architecture into an underwater structure to restore ecological habitat and local infrastructure. Hopkinson portrays the corals as agents in the reclamation of national sovereignty through the biological activity of quarrying seawater.

In another example of Black Atlantic futurity and corals, consider artist Ellen Gallagher's *Coral Cities* (2007). As part of her longer project *Watery Ecstatic*, Gallagher's works play with gothic configurations of underwater life that blur any easy division between the mineral (white bones, geologic structures) and the biological (polyps, flesh). The essays in the companion publication *Coral Cities* dwell extensively with Gallagher's referentiality to the Drexciya mythos—an underwater society descended from pregnant African women who drowned in the Middle Passage—exploring the aftermath of those who survived the graveyard of the Atlantic.[33] Yet neither essay in *Coral Cities* discusses the

32. Gemma Conroy, "Can Sculptures Help Coral Reefs Bounce Back?" https://hakaimagazine.com/news/can-sculptures-help-coral-reefs-bounce-back/.

33. On the gothic aesthetics of the underwater shipwreck and its atmosphere, see Margaret Cohen, *The Underwater Eye: How the Movie Camera Opened the Depths and Unleashed New Realms of Fantasy*

titular element of coral; so where does coral, in fact, lie? Perhaps Gallagher's coral cities exist not only in the aftermath of the underwater shipwreck but also in the polyp-like appearance of human faces, ringed by the circular accretions of magazine cut-outs; or through the way she delicately carves into bone-white paper, creating atoll-shaped cuts of more-than-human life that are barely visible in its photographic documentation—an effect better seen in person, through the contrast of a shadowed lighting. Or perhaps through the way Gallagher plays with embedding faces in green strands of something seaweed-like, each face ringed by tentacle-like white hair as if it were a new kind of coral polyp. Or perhaps through her watercolor paintings of medusa-like figures—coral mythologized, after all, as the blood of Medusa dripped into the sea—their textured white hair conjoining into an archipelago above them. *Coral Cities* contests where we might expect to find life, offering surprising forms of hybridity and mutation, inviting us to think about soft bodies, not only about stony forms. Her cities are architectures built *of* and *by* polyps with anthropomorphic features, polyps that might reach out across time to offer an affective sting.

(Princeton, N.J.: Princeton University Press, 2021), 11 and 120–21. Focusing on the documentaries of Jacques Cousteau, Cohen shows how their visual qualities—slanted camera angles, haziness, and Ann Radcliffe's articulation of "almost roofless walls"—were made possible by "by the physical qualities of the ocean environment" (121–22) such as buoyancy and opacity.

2. Softness

JUST PRIOR to the Covid-19 pandemic of 2020 I had the opportunity to visit Fiji, which is known in the scuba diving community as the soft coral capital of the world. One notable drift dive was at "Purple Haze," a site that was best visited during the changing of the daily tides. Purple Haze—referencing a Jimi Hendrix song—alluded to a particularly dense wall of violet soft corals that the incoming tide would cause to "bloom," the floral verb used to describe the inflation of their hydroskeletons. While there are many types of soft corals, this particular kind relied on the flux of the current to activate their bodies, so that they changed from an appearance of crushed tissue paper into softly ballooned branches, tufted with lavender polyps ready to grasp passing food particles. As I drifted along past this wall, I was aware that the currents enabling the corals to bloom also prevented me from pausing in place to examine the corals more closely. I could only observe them in motion, even as a few people in the group swam countercurrent to try to obtain photographs. Of course, divers present their own disturbances. Reflecting on another Fijian dive site, "Mellow Yellow," one person recalled how "dozens of divers circumnavigate popular pinnacles every day, their exhaust bubbles percolate upward and scrub the soft corals above. We may aspire to take only pictures and leave only bubbles, but on sites with vertical walls, overhangs or pinnacles, the bubbles may cause damage."[1]

Compared with stony corals, soft corals have received less scientific (and practically no humanistic) attention.[2] In the acknowledgments of *Soft Corals and Sea Fans* (2001), the editors write, "Until now, no comprehensive and user-friendly reference material to soft corals and sea fans of the warm shallow waters of the broader Indo-Pacific region existed."[3] Indeed, the section on soft corals in *The Biology of Reefs and Reef Organisms* (2013)—which one would expect to be a totalizing survey of many types of corals—is a mere two paragraphs long. Across textbooks and popular media forms, Corals largely imply reef-building stony corals, obscuring the variety of other types of corals and their near-kin relations.

Soft corals, together with sea fans, blue corals, and sea pens, are part of the animal group Octocorallia. The polyps of these organisms have eight tentacles, rather than six (as with stony corals, which are part of Hexacorallia).[4] Soft corals have no solid skeleton, although some have small internal structures called sclerites—like icicles made of calcium carbonate—unique to particular species. In lieu of a skeleton, some soft corals pump water through the mouths of their polyps into internal canals, forming a hydroskeleton that can be quickly inflated or deflated

1. Diver's Alert Network, "Fiji: Soft Coral Capital of the World," https://dan.org/alert-diver/article/fiji-soft-coral-capital-of-the-world/.

2. In one exception, Peter Godfrey-Smith dedicates a chapter in *Metazoa* to soft corals, locating the evolutionary beginnings of animal action in soft corals, "action that involves coordination across vast scales from a cell's point of view." Peter Godfrey-Smith, *Metazoa: Animal Life and the Birth of the Mind* (New York: Farrar, Straus, Giroux, 2020), 54.

3. Katharina Fabricius and Philip Alderslade, *Soft Corals and Sea Fans* (Durban, South Africa: Durban Natural Science Museum, 2001), v.

4. Fabricius and Alderslade, 1.

Figure 3. A diver pauses behind a roof of soft corals in Fiji. Photograph by Melody Jue, 2020.

as needed.[5] Soft corals are found in the Indo-Pacific Ocean but not the Atlantic, and colonies can be hundreds of years old.

If a dominant coralation has been to see Corals as builders—as architectural agents, as makers of worlds—what happens when we shift our consideration to soft corals? How do soft corals differ from the stony iconicity of Corals, exemplified in Shakespeare's

5. Fabricius and Alderslade, 14.

oft-cited passage from *The Tempest*, "Full fathom five thy father lies / Of his bones are corals made / Those are pearls that were his eyes"?[6] Whereas bleached corals have become iconic and gothic images of precarity in the face of ocean warming—bone-like in their depigmentation—what kind of narrative might we tell about soft corals in face of climate precarity? Are stony corals, in their evocation of bones, more mournable subjects?

To think with soft corals is to undo the normative coralation of Coral with building and the accretion of records. We encounter one such scene in the documentary film *Chasing Coral* (2017), directed by Jeff Orlowski, which dramatizes the effects of extreme ocean warming on coral reefs. *Chasing Coral* was planned as a sequel to *Chasing Ice* (2012), Orlowski's earlier documentary that followed a team that set up remote cameras to capture evidence of glacier recession over several months. Anticipating that a new ocean-warming event would lead to severe coral bleaching, Orlowski applied the same formula: set up underwater cameras to document the change from healthy corals to dead ones. However, *Chasing Coral* significantly varies from *Chasing Ice* through the failure of remote observation and recording. Despite best efforts to engineer automatic recording—underwater cameras inside glass globes, with a self-scraping mechanism for cleaning off algae—the cameras either died or produced blurry footage. With time running out, Orlowski and his team gave up on remote observation and instead opted for the labor-intensive option of scuba diving to make repeat observations of sites at Lizard Island, Australia. This was no vacation: diving involved the daily work of washing/drying heavy gear, pounds of weights, multiple tanks, and camera equipment. It was physically exhausting. Although Orlowski's team had planned for (and wanted) remote observa-

6. William Shakespeare, *The Tempest*, I.2.

tion, they found themselves committed to embodied observation, documenting the dying corals, both soft and stony, through daily submergences. These dives exemplify what it means to "dwell in the dissolve," Stacy Alaimo's term for the ecological grief of recognizing transcorporeal vulnerability.[7]

One scene at end of the documentary features an affective moment of soft coral contact. Coral enthusiast Zach Rapo gently disturbs the water around a necrosing coral with his hand, sending fleshy strands of mucus opaquely into the water. His extradiegetic narration adds, "It's flesh. It's living tissue . . . that's rotting away." He swims away to bring something back to show the camera for a close-up: a yellow piece of soft coral, nested in his two hands, disintegrating to produce a mucus-white halo. Unlike stony corals, whose bone-white skeletons remain after the polyps die, soft corals simply melt into the ocean, leaving no record of their existence. The scene then cuts to Rapo pulling out an underwater notebook and pencil, where he scrawls the sentence, "This is the hardest dive I've ever had to do," and holds it up to show the camera. *Chasing Coral* juxtaposes this familiar mode of inscription—writing on a tablet—with something that appears to be its antithesis: dissolution.

The fact that *Chasing Coral* centers on moments of dissolution lends it political urgency, but also draws coralations to the media form of the book. Consider the following metaphor used by Richard Vevers, who worked in advertising before turning his attention to ocean activism as the CEO of XL Catlin Seaview Survey: "Losing the Barrier Reef has got to mean something. You can't just let it die, and it becomes an old textbook. It's got to cause the change it deserves." This comparison to "an old textbook" initially struck me as odd, since it is still a type of

7. Stacy Alaimo, *Exposed: Environmental Politics and Pleasures in Posthuman Times* (Minneapolis: University of Minnesota Press, 2016).

record that endures. Yet it makes a certain sense if what the textbook lacks is a readership. Vevers wants coral death to "cause the change it deserves," to transform coral corpses from the realm of the abject back into the realm of signification—into inscriptions—that will catalyze action. This desire to catalyze change manifests in the structure of the documentary itself: *Chasing Coral* is the type of documentary that sets up the viewer to fulfill the very lack that it assumes from the beginning. If, by the end of the film, you find yourself feeling pathos for the corals, then you help the documentary achieve its goal—the invitation to care—which carefully avoids systemic critiques of capitalism, or energy-intensive video streaming of its Netflix distribution, aimed at a global North audience.[8]

But to return to Vevers's description of the reef as an old textbook: perhaps soft corals challenge another coralation, the imagination of Coral (stony corals, again) as a kind of inscriptive record of the past climate. During one moment in *Chasing Coral,* Dr. Neal Cantin opens a drawer full of thin, bone-white slabs. These slabs are samples of coral, that the documentary reminds us that "you can look at growth rings in corals in the same way you can look at growth rings in trees." I find it difficult to ignore the visual similarity between these coral samples and stony tablets, surfaces for (what are here read as) inscriptions of an oceanic climate record. Stony corals lend themselves so easily to media analogies with records, perhaps because of the temporal

8. See Mark Sweney, "Streaming's Dirty Secret: How Viewing Netflix Top 10 Creates Vast Quantity of CO2," *The Guardian,* October 29, 2021, https://www.theguardian.com/tv-and-radio/2021/oct/29/streamings-dirty-secret-how-viewing-netflix-top-10-creates-vast-quantity-of-co2. See also Laura U. Marks et al., "Streaming Media's Environmental Impact," *Media+Environment* 2, no. 1 (2020), https://mediaenviron.org/article/17242-streaming-media-s-environmental-impact.

linearity of how each residue of calcium carbonate accretes and hardens on top of another—like tree rings, or geologic strata. Cantin points out a normal growth pattern in one sample of 1.5 cm per year, until 1998, when bleaching due to an ocean warming event interrupts its formation—one of several interruptions caused by global climate change from anthropogenic carbon dioxide emissions. This kind of climate record is not possible to trace in the bodies of soft corals, which—in a non–book type of way—simply melt away into the ocean during extreme moments of heat stress.

Heat can be a difficult phenomenon to film because it is not primarily visual.[9] During the massive ocean heatwave in 2016 that *Chasing Coral* documents, a full third of all corals in the Great Barrier Reef were affected by bleaching. Bleaching is the stress response of the corals to extra-warm water, whereby they eject their symbiotic algae (zooxanthellae).[10] Losing these algae causes corals to lose pigment, resulting in the bleach-white color of bone in the stony corals. The bone-white skeletons left behind (such as those that adorn the cover of Irus Braverman's book, *Coral Whisperers: Scientists on the Brink* [2018]) make ocean warming visible as spectacular indexes, drawing a visual coralation between coral death and colorlessness. If coral skeletons attest to the accretion of time, then such a temporal record is endangered by the effects of coral bleaching and ocean acidification. Consider a striking metaphor from Allan Sekula in *Fish Story,* "the gum disease of the future eats away at the teeth of the

9. More specifically, heat is detectable in the infrared, just outside the spectrum of visible light, and shimmering heatwaves are a visual phenomenon specific to air.

10. Quirin Schiermeier, "Great Barrier Reef Saw Huge Losses from 2016 Heatwave," https://www.nature.com/articles/d41586-018-04660-w.

past."[11] Stony corals, like teeth, might also be said to suffer from the "gum disease" of anthropogenic climate change. More literally, anthropologist Amy Moran-Thomas moves past the figure of the mouth to notice a more digestive material metaphor in the case of corals, which are "showing signs of metabolic disorders" because of increasing heat stress, which causes starvation and bleaching.[12]

Here my thought drifts back to soft corals, which, instead of bleaching into a white skeleton during ocean warming events, simply *dissolve* under thermal stress. What media analogies do soft corals lend themselves to, if their fleshy materiality is so different from that of their stony cousins? What are the media of softness? These are questions that challenge the way that many scholars imagine the Anthropocene through print media. Theorizations of the Anthropocene commonly draw on a spatio-temporal logic of layering likened to chapters of Earth's history, a bookish comparison.[13] Consider how the Anthropocene has drifted toward analogies of writing, where humanity inscribes the next epoch of geologic history in Earth's strata—measurable by radioactive isotopes or by synthetic plastics packed into our ever-increasing trash heaps—or erases newly extinct species in the future fossil record. As Tobias Boes and Kate Marshall write,

11. Allan Sekula, *Fish Story* (London: Mack Books, 2018), 150. My thanks to Caio Santos for this reference.

12. Amy Moran-Thomas, "Sweetness across Thresholds at the Edge of the Sea," in *Eating Beside Ourselves*, ed. Heather Paxson (Durham, N.C.: Duke University Press, 2023), 37.

13. "In the same way, everywhere on Earth, traces of earlier epochs persist in the contours of landforms and the rocks beneath, even as new chapters are being written. The discipline of geology is akin to an optical device for seeing the Earth text in all its dimensions." Marcia Bjornerud, *Timefulness: How Thinking Like a Geologist Can Help Save the World* (Princeton, N.J.: Princeton University Press, 2018), 22.

"The Anthropocene makes Lascaux painters out of all of us, for we all collectively inscribe messages upon our planet that our distant descendants (provided they exist) will one day approach with wonderment and incomprehension."[14] Even though we can read records of the climate in the stony bodies of some corals, this tactic does not work in the case of immediately felt effects like ocean heat. Geological strata are but one body, or one medium, for the Anthropocene to register.

What is the Anthropocene for soft corals? Perhaps a matter of saturation. As Rafico Ruiz and I wrote in our introduction to *Saturation: An Elemental Politics* (2021), saturation evokes both a watery and chemical poetics. While the *Oxford English Dictionary* defines *saturation* as the feeling of being "full" or "glutted," we also might think of a saturated solution in a chemistry lab.[15] Saturation offers a trans-elemental imaginary that "positions scholars to compare materials and social forces that might not otherwise find themselves in the same conversation," modeling an important alternative to (not a total replacement of) the popular concept of entanglement—which is more suggestive of threads, yarns, or vines, and implies the possibility of disentanglement.[16] The Anthropocene oceans are saturated by political decisions and petrocultural dependency that drive global climate change and extreme ocean-warming events. But saturation also comes to matter in the liveliness of soft coral bodies; recall that seawater is the milieu that sustains soft corals as their tentacles slowly grasp and unfold in the current, the water forming their

14. Tobias Boes and Kate Marshall, "Writing the Anthropocene: An Introduction," *Minnesota Review,* no. 83, special issue, "Writing the Anthropocene," ed. Tobias Boes and Kate Marshall (2014): 63.

15. Melody Jue and Rafico Ruiz, eds., *Saturation: An Elemental Politics* (Durham, N.C.: Duke University Press, 2021), 1.

16. Jue and Ruiz, 4.

hydroskeleton—in this state, they are (following the OED) full and glutted with water. When we think about all the ways that seawater is both inside and outside the soft corals, buoying them, assisting in coral reproduction, carrying nutrients, and how corals are sensitive to changes in current, it is harder to hold onto an ontological division between organism and environment, coral and ocean. Soft corals necessitate attention to the prepositional mode of being "of" the ocean, not as builders erecting lasting edifices, but as fluid sculptures of flowing water.

If soft corals had been the dominant reef organism that Darwin and other British explorers encountered, I wonder if it would have been as tempting to coralate them with metaphors of empire and empire building. Where stony corals blur the ontological categories of animal, vegetable, and mineral, soft corals offer more distance from the mineral (although some varieties, as I mentioned, build sclerites). Descriptions of soft corals drift more toward *plants* rather than *architectures* (soft corals "blooming" or forming "gardens"), comparisons that channel gendered correlations between softness and femininity, or gardening as a woman's activity—an exception being Bronislaw Malinowski's *Coral Gardens and their Magic* (1935), which references stony reefs in the Trobriand Islands. In *Chasing Coral,* soft corals do not suggest permanent records but rather forms of ephemerality, fleshy bodies that decompose as easily as tree leaves into the heat of a compost pile.

3. Coldness

WHERE SOFT CORALS offer the surprise of fleshiness athwart the stony iconicity of Coral, cold-water corals offer the surprise of thriving in the chill of the deep. Indeed, the coralation between corals and tropical habitats has dominated the public imaginary and remains the focus of scientific attention. Nearly all global maps of corals, and coral textbooks, focus on tropical corals. The massive Allen Coral Atlas, for example, purports to "map the world's coral reefs," yet includes data on tropical corals alone.[1] One deep-sea biologist with whom I spoke said that he had never been asked to peer review any tropical coral research, while warm-water coral biologists regularly peer review cold-water coral research.[2] It is perhaps unsurprising, then, that the humanities have followed suit and focused book-length studies almost exclusively on warm-water, stony (scler-actinian), reef-building (hermatypic) corals—their mediations, endangerment, and symbiotic relations.[3] What kinds of expec-

1. Allen Coral Atlas, https://allencoralatlas.org/.
2. Eric Cordes, personal email, 2022.
3. With the exception of Bergemark and Jørgenson "*Lophelia pertusa* Conservation in the North Sea Using Obsolete Offshore Structures as Artificial Reefs" (2014) and parts of coral biologist Malcolm Shick's

tations do cold-water corals break, and what kind of new coralations do they put into perspective?

While many species of cold-water corals exist throughout the
world, one widespread species in the Atlantic Ocean is *Lophelia
pertusa*.[4] *Lophelia* is found as shallow as two-hundred feet under
the sea in cold waters off the coast of Norway, as well as thousands of feet deep in the Gulf of Mexico and off the continental
shelf of West Africa. The Oxford English Dictionary defines a
reef as a "ridge or bank of rock, sand, shingle, etc., lying just
above or just below the surface of the sea or another body of
water, usually in such a way as to pose a hazard to shipping."[5]
This definition, linking reefs with surface-level hazards, risks
leaving out reefs of Lophelia, since many are too deep to cause
shipwrecks. Geographically, one of the largest reefs of *Lophelia*
in the world is Røst Reef, off the coast of Norway. Unlike tropical corals that live close to the surface and bright sunlight, the
deep-water environments preferred by cold-water corals are
quite dark. Acclimated to an environment without sun, *Lophelia*
is azooxanthellate—existing without symbiotic algae, whose metabolism depends on photosynthesizing sunlight.[6] Susan Milius
playfully calls Lophelia "corals without boarders," a homophonic

---

excellent visual history *Where the Corals Lie* (2018), JSTOR did not turn
up any other results.

4. *Lophelia pertusa* was recently renamed *Desmophyllum pertu-
sum* in the World Register of Marine Species (WoRMS), in response to
molecular studies by Addamo et al. in 2012 and 2016. However, I have
chosen to retain the Linnean name, which is still widely recognized
and was used in primary source material I quote from circa 2019. See:
https://www.marinespecies.org/aphia.php?p=taxdetails&id=135161.

5. "Reef," Oxford English Dictionary

6. On tropical corals and metabolism, see Cameron McKean,
http://somatosphere.net/2020/life-coral-body-great-barrier-reef.html/.

pun on "borders."[7] Due to its lack of zooxanthellae, *Lophelia* is nearly colorless, taking its name from *lophos* (tuft of) and *helios* (sun) to describe the bright white tufted polyps that adorn its branches, feeding by grasping particles of food that float by in the water column. Thus, one key coralation that *Lophelia* breaks is the way coral implies symbiosis—a relationship that Irus Braverman highlights in her discussion of coralations: "The symbiotic algae-microbes-animal relationship at the core of the corals' precarious existence reveals that, more than a single unified entity, corals are 'coralations'—bundles of constantly changing associations that shape and reshape their ways of being in the world and, therefore, the world itself."[8] Because of the way that *Lophelia* deviates from dominant coralations with symbiosis, sunlight, color, and tropicality, it was described by one textbook as "the coral that breaks all the rules."[9]

One implication of deviating from expectations of symbiosis is that *Lophelia* exists in different relations to environmental mediation. Whereas tropical corals lend themselves to photographic analogies, cold-water corals do not. Consider the way that Ann Elias—reflecting on the early twentieth-century photography of John Williamson and Frank Hurley—describes the way that both corals and photographic practices rely on light:

A thoroughly modern relationship developed between photography and filmmaking, coral reefs, and tropical water, one based in the common ingredient of light and the material quality of transparency. It became apparent that there was a magical correspondence in the way the natural phenomenon of corals and

7. Susan Milius, "Corals without Boarders," *Science News* 166, no. 6 (2004): 88–89.

8. Braverman, *Coral Whisperers*, 1.

9. Roberts 1997, quoted in Martin Hovland, *Deep-Water Coral Reefs: Unique Biodiveresity Hot-Spots* (New York: Springer, 2008), ix.

the technological processes of photographs both required light for photochemical reactions. It was a revelation that corals, as well as photographs, needed light to bring them to life and enable development.[10]

This passage about the importance of light in the lifeworlds of corals and photography resonates with the way that Erin Despard and Michael Gallagher define "photomedia" as a "strategic abstraction that enables us to identify visual relations in which plants and cameras alike are implicated."[11] In the case of tropical corals, symbiotic algae are the "plants" that are photosensitive to light and assist in the growth and development of the coral. Here, the word *development* slides between biological and photographic valences, enabling an easy relation between developing an image and developing as a lifeform. In addition, Elias goes on to show how, for Williamson and Hurley, the remarkable *clarity* of Caribbean and Australian seawater served as a kind of technical extension of the camera lens, air-like and providing a slight magnification. Even in artificial situations, like aquarium dioramas, glass and seawater are often seen as continuous extensions of each other that mediate the visual perception of tropical corals.

Stories about *Lophelia* suggest a different relation to glass, through sound rather than vision. Engineer and marine geologist Martin Hovland provides one striking example in his textbook *Deep-Water Coral Reefs: Unique Biodiversity Hot-spots* (2008). Hovland recounts a memory from a cruise in July 1982, when—as an employee of the Norwegian company Statoil—he was mapping the seafloor while aboard the survey vessel *Master Surveyor* for a future oil pipeline from the Åskeladden field in the Barents

10. Elias, *Coral Empire,* 20.
11. Erin Despard and Michael Gallagher, "The Media Ecologies of Plant Invasion," *Environmental Humanities* 10, no. 2 (2018): 373.

Sea to Lyngenfjord, Norway. Through the use of sidescan sonar, Hovland noticed an unusual, cone-shaped structure on the seafloor, hundreds of meters below. He directed the crew to use a gravity corer to sample the site:

> Soon, the corer hovered at 260 metres depth, right above the top of the unidentified strange cone. Suddenly the corer was dropped until the wire went slack. As it was winched in, excitement rose. Most of us expected just another sticky clay core. *But we had luck and a sigh of astonishment went round as several pieces of white coral bits fell tinkling onto the steel deck, it sounded like bits of glass falling* [my emphasis].[12]

Although the first description of the *Lophelia* sample is visual ("white coral bits fell . . ."), the analogy to glass emphasizes its *acoustic* properties rather than its visual clarity. *Lophelia* is sensed through almost musical register, echoing through contact with the steel floor of the petroleum survey ship. This moment of direct mediation builds on the circumstances of distant and technical mediation that led Hovland to the site in the first place: the acoustic technology of sonar, which so effectively transduces sound into visual data for ship navigation and seafloor sensing.[13] Whereas visuality is primary in assessing tropical coral reefs, sound—specifically the technical mediation of sonar—is the medium that allows surveyors to see through the opacity of the ocean toward cold-water corals, even thousands of feet deep.

Lophelia recalibrates our iconic expectations of Coral through its geographic distribution in deep and cold waters, its media relations, and—importantly—the new coralation it presents with proximity to infrastructures of petroleum ex-

12. Hovland, *Deep-Water Coral Reefs*, 16.
13. On "transductive ethnography" see Stefan Helmreich, *Alien Ocean: Anthropological Voyages in Microbial Seas* (Los Angeles: University of California Press, 2009), 230.

traction. Like the coast of Norway, the geographies mentioned earlier where *Lophelia* lives—the Gulf of Mexico and western coast of Africa—are also sites of oil extraction. Although many scientists favor the conservation of deep sea ecologies, the oil industry sometimes volunteers submersible time for scientific research, since it has the expensive vessels that are able to reach deep and remote sites.[14] In the context of Norway, there is also a history of cooperation between Norwegian fishermen and oil companies, even though *Lophelia* reefs are important nurseries for juvenile fish, which if damaged could impact future fisheries.[15] One system of nine live reefs—the oldest of which is 8,150 years old—was named after an oil pipeline, and became Haltenpipe Reef Cluster (HRC).[16]

Some scientists have debated the question: does the geographic correlation between seafloor oil seeps and *Lophelia* also include an aspect of *causation*? Do *Lophelia* reefs metabolically benefit from nearby oil seeps? Hovland—an engineer by training—argues that there is such an element of causation in what he calls a "hydraulic theory," which holds that *Lophelia*'s "wellbeing and proliferation [. . .] relies on the assumption that there is a stable, local input of nutrients through the seabed at or near the location where the reefs are found," and that oil seeps provide these nutrients.[17] For Hovland, the geographical proximity of *Lophelia* to soil seeps should not be overlooked. Studies from the Gulf of Mexico arrive at other conclusions, suggesting that *Lophelia* may

14. For example, Cindy Van Dover, "Tighten Regulations on Deep-Sea Mining," *Nature* 470, 31–33 (2011), https://doi.org/10.1038/470031a.

15. Elena Parmiggiani and Eric Monteiro, "Digitized Coral Reefs," in *digitalSTS: A Field Guide for Science and Technology Studies,* ed. Vertesi et al. (Princeton, N.J.: Princeton University Press, 2019).

16. Hovland, *Deep-Water Coral Reefs,* 46.

17. Hovland and Risk, "Do Norwegian Deep-Water Coral Reefs Rely on Seeping Fluids?" *Marine Geology* 198 (2003): 84.

favor the rocky substrates that are the byproduct of gas-eating microbes, the type of rocky perch that may be advantageous for filtering food particles. Oceanographer Eric Cordes writes that the geological formations left by previous seeps could make favorable sites for *Lophelia* to grow: "These hardgrounds are colonized by deep-sea corals, and could be considered the final successional stage of a seep community."[18] Further, biologist Erin Becker found that, "while coral communities shared several of the same animals found at seep communities, the tissue stable isotope values of the coral and its inhabitants did not reflect a strong signature characteristic of a gas-fueled ecosystem" because "the signatures of the carbonate rock it settled upon were different from *Lophelia*'s skeleton indicating that it was derived from gas-fueled or other microbial processes."[19] If these studies in the Gulf of Mexico are correct, then coralation is not causation; oil seeps do not cause *Lophelia* to grow. The one exception might be when Lophelia decides to settle on oil platforms as artificial reefs, as Paulina Bergemark and Dolly Jørgenson have noted.[20]

We can trace different material coralations between *Lophelia* and petroleum extraction in the crochet installation "Coral Forest," commissioned for the 2021 Helsinki Biennial (themed "The Same Sea") in Finland—a handicraft variation on "soft" coral from the previous chapter, here made entirely of yarn. "Coral Forest" was an iteration of Christine and Margaret Wertheim's Hyperbolic Crochet Coral Reef, a collaborative artwork whose scale and multitude of participants often draw comparisons to

18. Eric Cordes, "The Ecology of Gulf of Mexico Deep-Sea Hardground Communities," https://oceanexplorer.noaa.gov /explorations/06mexico/background/hardgrounds/hardgrounds.html.

19. Kevin Zelnio, "Deep Sea Corals and Methane Seeps," https:// deepseanews.com/2009/07/seeps-lophelia-carbonate-2/.

20. Bergemark and Jørgenson "*Lophelia pertusa* Conservation in the North Sea Using Obsolete Offshore Structures as Artificial Reefs."

the AIDS quilt. The reef embodies a form of feminist handicraft that celebrates the similarities in form between ocean organisms and crocheted shapes, which both embody the mathematics of non-Euclidian geometry inspired by mathematician Daina Taimiṇa. As anthropologist Sophia Roosth notes, "Reef crafters, while following her technique, use her algorithm as a starting point from which to digress and upon which to embellish in order to yield what they consider to be 'biological' forms."[21] While the initial reefs were crocheted by the Wertheim sisters, subsequent projects ("satellite reefs") have involved thousands of participants from around the world. More than three thousand Finnish people participated in contributing pieces to the Helsinki reef. Environmental humanities scholar Heather Davis describes this collaborative process as one in which "each person becomes part of a wider whole, analogous to an individual coral 'polyp,' engaging with the slow process of building a collective form."[22] Here, "community and individual agency are activated, mirroring the formation of living reefs that also grow in relation to their local conditions."[23]

To see a brightly colored coral reef sculpture in a Scandinavian environment might seem to exemplify the dominant coralation between coral and the rainbow tropics. Wouldn't it be more appropriate to commission a reef emulating cold-water corals, like *Lophelia pertusa* (though still some distance from the Baltic Sea), that are geographically closer to Finland than their warm-water

21. Sophia Roosth, "Evolutionary Yarns in Seahorse Valley: Living Tissues, Wooly Textiles, Theoretical Biologies," *differences* 25, no. 5 (2012): 15.

22. Heather Davis, "Feeling Crochet, Feeling Coral," in Margaret and Christine Wertheim, *Value and Transformation of Corals: Catalogue for the Exhibition at Museum Frieder Burda 2022* (Cologne, Germany: Weinand Verlag, 2022), 31.

23. Davis, 31.

cousins? Why emulate the rainbow colors of the tropics instead? While the Helsinki Coral Forest may not represent cold-water corals, it doesn't exactly represent warm-water corals either. The corals are much more fantastic—coral-like without always representing specific species—with crocheters positioned to evolve and *fabricate* new forms. Reflecting on some of the earlier Hyperbolic Crochet Coral Reefs, Roosth examines the conditions under which the Reef's makers "describe their work in explicitly biological terms [...] to claim that they are fabricating new taxa, new genera, new species [...]."[24] We might see the Helsinki Coral Forest as precisely such a fabrication rather than a representation of corals, uncoralated from the species that make their home in the cold waters of the North Atlantic.

If we think of fabrication in terms of material, it is also significant that the Helsinki Reef was made from repurposed petroleum-based plastics. The corals take on fantastical colors and forms, including highlights of "printer's ink" and "bluish-violet," from upcycled strips of plastic leftover from toilet paper packaging, among other materials.[25] In several corals, bands of white and purple spiral across crenellated forms, along with an anemone-like creature with lime-green zip ties for tentacles. The shine on the reef belies its plastic form, across so many crevices created by the crochet stiches. The textured forms of donated and repurposed plastic strips draw attention to what many purchased yarns made of acrylic or polyester hide: the fact that these common yarns are also made of petroleum-based plastics (constituting, for example, the majority of the yarns carried by the local Michael's craft store where I live in the United States).

24. Roosth, "Evolutionary Yarns in Seahorse Valley," 11.
25. Margaret Wertheim and Christine Wertheim, *Value and Transformation of Corals*, 99.

To crochet a reef out of plastic strips formally echoes the coralation of *Lophelia* reefs and petroleum infrastructures.

Climate change amplifies other coralations with petroleum. During the unusually hot and rainy summer of 2021, the plastic reef exhibit took a turn for the worse: "On Vallisaari, the island where the artworks were displayed, the bunkers became infested with mold. Video screens dripped with slime, projectors burnt out; but these were solvable problems. For the corals, a more permanent tragedy ensued. Blobs of mold blossomed on the pedestals and on the understructures holding up the works."[26] Reflecting on the way that the rise in summer temperatures was part of the ongoing rise in global temperatures fueled by increased atmospheric carbon from global oil extraction, the Wertheims write: "Even plastic sea creatures can't stand the onslaught of humanity's petrochemical ensorcellment."[27] Although the crochet reefs had been intended to be shown next in Germany, the presence of mold meant that international shipping could not happen. The Wertheims wryly comment that if the corals had been made by a more famous artist (Anish Kapoor or Jeff Koons, for example) a way forward could have been found; the decision to throw away the artworks likely reflected a broader devaluation of multiartist craftworks. Parallel to how oceanic sea creatures face threats from ocean warming and plastic pollution, the plastic sea creatures were made disposable by the growth of molds. The coralation between Scandinavian reefs and petromodernity remains coincident in both living corals and abstract forms, *Lophelia pertusa* and hyperbolic crochet, each under threat of unraveling.

26. Wertheim and Wertheim, 101.
27. Wertheim and Wertheim, 101.

4. Grafting

I NOW TURN TO a different type of stitching—not of crochet yarn but of photographs in the diptychs of Vincentian artist Nadia Huggins.[1] So far, *Coralations* has focused on exceptional corals that break common expectations about iconic Coral. Where Huggins goes further is through using corals and other marine organisms to disrupt acculturated habits of reading the gendered body in physical space. Huggins's series *Transformations* (2014–2016) challenges habits of orientation and visual interpretation through a series of photographic self-portraits matched with oceanic environments and lifeforms. In her photography, corals are not just the subjects of coralations, but the *agents*. In particular, Huggins juxtaposes corals as extensions of limbs, shoulders, and faces (like the surrealist game "the exquisite corpse"). Through grafting marine contours to the human form, Huggins's photography breaks normative coralations of how bodies are read in terms of gender, age, and race.

In a TEDx talk in 2017 entitled, "What's Beyond the Shoreline?" Huggins describes the experience of identifying

1. I have Maria Molano Parrado to thank for connecting me with Nadia Huggins's photograph during the summer course I taught on "Coral Mediations" at the University of Bologna in 2022.

as a woman while growing up with alopecia, and how she was often read as a boy because of her loss of hair.[2] Huggins was born in Trinidad and Tobago and grew up in St. Vincent and the Grenadines, where she is currently based. Taking her camera underwater, she began to observe the ways in which the experience of immersing in the ocean assisted in undoing, or at least confusing, normative perceptions of gender. In *Is that a buoy?* (2015), Huggins puns on the homophone of "buoy/boy," juxtaposing a black-and-white self-portrait of a buoy next to another portrait of her partially submerged head.[3] The visual similarity between the two forms invites misreading, as well as a second look: the hint of an eyebrow, the faint wisp of an eyelash. Huggins writes that her photographs explore "the ambiguity of the body in the sea, especially when observed from a distance, and the assumptions one makes about gender and sexuality based on physical appearances [. . .] I am stereotyped as being masculine constantly because of the absence of my hair."[4] In the series *Circa no future* (2014 and ongoing), Huggins swam close to a group of boys who were taking turns jumping into the water, where they assumed she was just another boy.[5] When she got close

2. Nadia Huggins, "What's Beyond the Boundary of the Shoreline?" https://www.ted.com/talks/nadia_huggins_what_s_beyond_the_boundary_of_the_shoreline.

3. In another cultural pun on buoy/boy, consider this verse from Kate Bush's "And Dream of Sheep": "Little light shining / Little light will guide them to me / My face is all lit up / My face is all lit up / If they find me racing white horses / They'll not take me for a buoy." My thanks to Stefan Helmreich for the reference.

4. Nadia Huggins, "Is That a Buoy?" https://nadiahuggins.com/Is-that-a-buoy.

5. Elizabeth Deloughrey and Tatiana Flores, "Submerged Bodies: The Tidalectics of Representability and the Sea in Caribbean Art," *Environmental Humanities* 12, no. 1 (2020): 152: "In a conversation with one of the authors, Huggins explained that the first time she swam

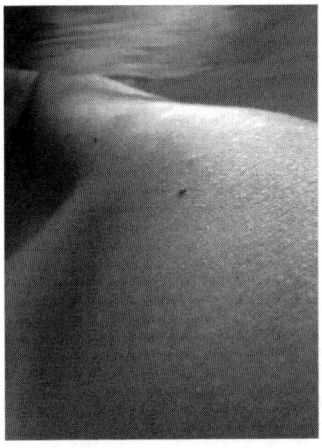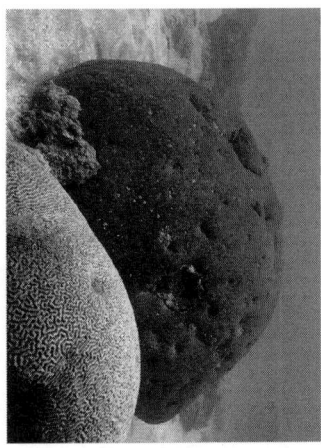

Figure 4. Nadia Huggins, "Transformations 3."

enough to photograph them, using an "unintrusive point and shoot" camera, she noticed that while their postures reflected normative forms of masculinity as they sat on the rocks—upright and angular—their bodies completely relaxed underneath the surface.[6] As Elizabeth Deloughrey and Tatiana Flores reflect, channeling Huggins, "despite themselves, the boys' performance of masculinity is dissolved in oceanic water."[7]

It is this potential for oceanic immersion to offer the experience of relaxing acculturated habits of embodiment that focuses Huggins's series *Transformations,* featuring diptychs of her underwater self-portraits juxtaposed with corals and other oceanic

toward the boys they assumed that she was also a boy so they behaved in a manner that was wholly free of constraint. When they noticed that she was female, they began posturing."

6. Deloughrey and Flores, 152; Nadia Huggins, "What's Beyond the Boundary of the Shoreline?"

7. Deloughrey and Flores, "Submerged Bodies," 152.

organisms.[8] Building on her reflections on gender and comportment in *Circa no future* and *Is that a buoy?*, which were created during the same time period, Huggins writes of *Transformations*: "In the sea, as a woman who identifies as other, my body becomes displaced from my everyday experiences. Gender, race, and class are dissolved because there are no social and political constructs to restrain and dictate my identity. These constructs have no place or value in that environment. This idea creates the foundation for these portraits."[9] This is not to say that the constructs of race, gender, and class always disappear underwater in visual media[10]—rather, I read Huggins as theorizing from her own somatic experience of floating in the water, and how oceanic dehabituation comes to bear on her artistic composition of *self-portraits* that include marine creatures.

While Huggins refers to the diptychs in *Transformations* as collages, I want to think also of the way that they involve processes of grafting. Grafting is a common practice in coral conservation, where fragments of living coral are attached to underwater rocks or other structures—a botanical technique for seeding future reefs. This technique was inspired by the observation that after a destructive event like a hurricane, some broken coral fragments could begin to regrow and regenerate from living tips. By analogy, what kinds of growth might we imagine from Huggins's photo-grafted, multispecies extensions of the human form submerged underwater?

8. In *Wild Blue Media* (2020), I also discuss the potential of the ocean as an environment for drawing attention to normative habits of embodiment formed in terrestrial contexts.

9. Nadia Huggins, *Transformations,* https://nadiahuggins.com /Transformations.

10. For example, Ann Elias notes the common racialization and gendering of the prone horizontal body in early twentieth-century photography; see for example chapter 10 of *Coral Empire*.

Before I explore this question, I want to note that Huggins's diptychs are formally different from other underwater photography of the human form and corals, perhaps most famously the underwater sculptures of Jason de Caires Taylor. At first glance, Taylor's photographs might seem more posthuman through the materiality of marine growth on human sculptural forms. Yet Taylor's underwater sculptures are nearly all shot as portraits, as if the photographer were standing on the seafloor, just as they would stand on land. As I write in *Wild Blue Media: Thinking through Seawater* (2020), the orientation of such portraiture reflects a terrestrial experience of gravity, rather than other possible oceanic conditions of viewing: floating overhead or being swept along one's side by changing currents.[11] Although Huggins's photographs also feature vertical orientations of the human on the left portrait in the diptych, they are always juxtaposed with a vertically flipped orientation of the coral or other marine organism on the right. Her formal choice to rotate the marine images by ninety degrees raises the question: when each pair of photographs is seen together, where is viewer in relation to the surface of the ocean? Specifically, how to read the white gap between the human and the oceanic lifeform?

This question of "where is the surface?" becomes especially important when we consider how Huggins's photographs deny perhaps the signature aspect of portraits: the human face. Through strategic cropping, Huggins creates self-portraits that are always partial aspects of her body, featuring perhaps just a shoulder, or a side view of her head that stops at the ear, the back of her hand—or if including her face, making sure it is backlit into undiscernible shadow. Grafted to these partial views of her body are marine extensions—urchins, sponges, brain corals, rocks encrusted with marine invertebrates—seen askew. Each

11. Jue, *Wild Blue Media*, 146–52.

grafting is carefully placed in a way that matches borders and colors to match Huggins's skintone and contours, producing the perhaps uncanny visual sensation of new kinds of living form. As Deloughrey and Flores write, "Huggins adopts a kind of diffractional ethics that eschews the unmarked observer and instead positions herself in relation to her subjects, considering her impact on their behavior and their interface."[12] Here, the interface is the graft between Huggins and each marine organism, a pluripotent site of identity formation. These are chimeric diptychs, photo-graftings which suture two forms into an emergent compound being.

I want to suggest that Huggins's marine photography is more trans-human in the prepositional sense of the prefix *trans-* (using the tilde, not the dash) that Adela C. Licona and Eva Hayward theorize[13]—rather than Ray Kurzweil's obsession with transcending the body. For Licona and Hayward, the prefix *trans-* draws from a double reference to transsexuality and the transoceanic, which they describe as "a crossing of spacetime, a movement within relationship," and a "refusing to dissolve difference in favor of recognizing coalitional modes of emergence as possibilities."[14] In Huggins's photography, the gap between the two portraits in each diptych is precisely what holds such trans-human difference, and directionality, open. Huggins reflects on the gap in the following way:

> This space represents a transient moment where I am regaining buoyancy and separating from the underwater environment to resurface. My intention with these photographs is to create a

12. Deloughrey and Flores, "Submerged Bodies," 157.
13. Adela C. Licona and Eva S. Hayward, "Trans-Waters-Coalitional Thinking on Art + Environment," https://www.terrain.org/2014/currents/trans-waters-coalitional-thinking-on-art-and-environment/.
14. Licona and Hayward.

lasting breath that defies human limitation. The transformation exists within the space in between photographs. It is in this moment that the viewer makes the decision if both worlds are able to separate or merge.[15]

Huggins suggests that we interpret each gap between photos not only spatially but temporally—a "transient moment" where she is about to "resurface." She figures each temporal gap as a "a lasting breath" between moments or images. It is this breath or pause that Huggins imagines is shared with the viewer, who is positioned to decide if both air and ocean worlds "are able to separate or merge." It also leaves open the directionality of time: are we to read the photographs left to right, or right to left? Is the human becoming-oceanic in a trajectory to further submerge underwater, or are oceanic lifeforms merging into a human body that is about to surface?

The photograph I am particularly struck by is "Transformations No. 3," which features a close-up of Huggins's bare shoulder—close enough to see soft creases and small moles. The image cuts off just before we see her the curve of her deltoid, which is visually completed by the juxtaposition of a round lobe of yellowish-green brain coral in the right portrait. The alignment of collarbone into a rounded shoulder of brain coral is perfectly matched, a graft of marine organism onto human form—or, to take Huggins's own reflections seriously—perhaps a detachment or budding of the brain coral *off of* the human form. The gap is what leaves both interpretive possibilities open. The fact that this is brain coral also matters, suggesting a relocation or exteriorization of cognition out of the head and onto the hub of an appendage. Such an arrangement is evocative of octopuses, which have both a brain and significant clusters of neurons at

15. Huggins, "Transformations."

the base of each arm. For a brain-like structure to exist in the shoulder suggests a new hierarchy of thought, not centered behind an expressive human face but in the mechanical hinge of an appendage prior to movement—a coincidence, perhaps, of the limb and the limbic.

Huggins's photo-grafts in *Transformations* model how cultural correlations—of the gendered body, of embodied thought—can be undone by corals through the grafts of photographic collage. This is a different kind of grafting than we normally see in conservation discourses. Whereas the conservationist goal of coral grafting focuses on reproducing coral through fragmentation as a solution to diminishing reefs, in Huggins's work, it is the human body that we see in fragments and parts, juxtaposed with larger corals and other underwater formations. But it is important to remember that these are self-portraits extended by the oceanic other. The grafting of human fragment and oceanic lifeform is both intimate and disorienting, calling into question the location of the artwork: where is the ocean's surface and to what horizon do we orient? In my view, it is possible that the oceanic surface is in the middle of the diptychs—the very gap of separation between images that Huggins calls a "lasting breath that defies human limitation," and within which the viewer might dwell for an impossible duration.

5. Optimization

IN SCIENTIFIC DISCOURSE, many corals are called "colonial organisms," a term for denoting the ontological ambiguity between the individual polyp and the community of many to which it metabolically belongs. However, this usage risks becoming an instance of what Mark Rifkin calls "settler common sense," a normalization of the word "colonial" detached from its broader associations with Indigenous dispossession and empire building.[1] Consider the possible alternatives for describing the multiplicity of coral being: coral as collectivity, coral as assemblage, or even coral as socialist. *Coralations* has examined artworks and narratives that center such forms of multiplicity, from the community project of crocheting the Hyperbolic Coral Reef to Nadia Huggins's practice of collage in her photographic diptychs, and the coral colonization of cruise ships in Nalo Hopkinson's "Repatriation." In this chapter, I turn to photo mosaics.

I have elsewhere argued that the mosaic names not only a form of art, but a particular epistemic practice in the ocean

1. Mark Rifkin, "Settler Common Sense," *Settler Colonial Studies* 3, no. 3–4 (2013): 322–40.

sciences.[2] One of the most common modes of surveying coral reefs—tropical or deep-water—is through taking high-resolution photographs and then digitally stitching them into a larger photomosaic. For example, the University of Miami, supported by the U.S. Strategic Environmental Research and Development Program (SERDP), has developed software tools for generating underwater landscape mosaics from both video and photographic coral reef surveys.[3] This method of surveying has much higher resolution than, say, taking a single photograph from closer to the surface, which would have to see through a larger volume of opaque seawater. Scripps Institution of Oceanography has a long-term monitoring project located on Palmyra Atoll, creating a time-series of more than one thousand photoquadrats of benthic reefs. The images were then manually traced in Photoshop, outlining "the borders of all live hard coral colonies, algal patches (i.e., turf, crustose coralline algae, and macroalgae separately), and any other benthic components—including soft corals and other invertebrates, within each photoquadrat. All organisms were then identified to the finest possible taxonomic resolution with a corresponding swatch color indicating their genus, species, or functional group."[4] The resulting abstractions look a bit like the pattern of camouflage in rainbow hues, ready for computational analysis through the careful preparation of hand-

2. Melody Jue, "'Pixels May Lose Kelp Canopy': The Photomosaic as Epistemic Figure for the Satellite Mapping and Modeling of Seaweeds," *Media+Environment* 3, no. 2 (2021), https://doi.org/10.1525/001c.21261.

3. "High Resolution Landscape Mosaics for Coral Reef Mapping and Monitoring," https://nmsfloridakeys.blob.core.windows.net/floridakeys-prod/media/archive/review/documents/ermosaicscoralmonitoring.pdf.

4. Scripps Institution of Oceanography, "Long-Term Monitoring of Benthic Coral Reef Communities," https://coralreefecology.ucsd.edu/long-term-monitoring-of-benthic-coral-reef-communities/.

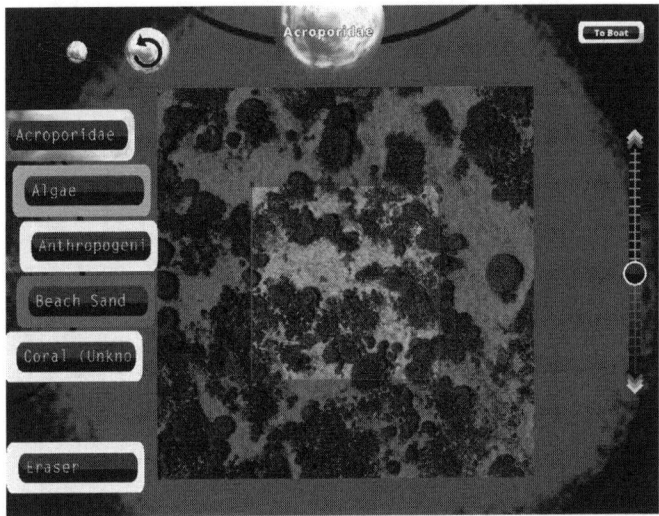

Figure 5. The interface of NeMO-Net, a game for teaching an algorithm to identify corals, screenshot.

tracing corals. These are but two examples of a common practice of photomosaic reef surveyal, either involving underwater photography conducted by scuba divers, or drone and satellite imaging through clear waters.

The challenge with this type of photomosaic survey is, how to count all the coral in the images? What to do with the mass of survey data? One gamified solution to the backlog of uncategorized coral photomosaics is the NASA-funded project NeMO-NET (Figure 5), a "a single player iPad game where players help NASA classify coral reefs by painting 3D and 2D images of coral."[5] Because the process of hand-identifying coral species or types is

---

5. NeMO-NET, http://nemonet.info/. My thanks to Colin Milburn for the reference.

slow and laborious, players—interpolated as citizen scientists—are invited to collectively participate in this work. Whereas some institutions collect photographs via diver surveys, NASA acquired the images of coral through drones and satellites, assisted by an algorithm called "fluid lensing," which edits away the distortions of seawater, mathematically erasing the opacity of the ocean so that it can be seen as if through air. This type of remote sensing assisted by AI processing is an example of what, in *Wild Blue Media,* I call a "terrestrial bias" calibrated to a human observer, whose normative environment is air rather than water. Even in air, vision is always a matter of mediation, a condition that is especially noticeable for human beings descending into underwater environments.[6] The images in the database of NeMO-NET are not so much about immersing humans in underwater worlds as they are about bringing underwater corals into the air-based *Umwelt* of human beings, a precondition for their surveyal and classification.

NeMO-NET also presents a new subject of coralation: the algorithm. As players progress through the game, identifying corals, their actions contribute to teaching a neural network how to better identify thousands of photographic images of coral reefs: "Data from the NeMO-Net game is fed to NASA NeMO-Net, the first neural multi-modal observation and training network for

---

6. In his essay "Looking Through the Surface" in *Liquid Door,* D. Graham Burnett asks why we can't see clearly underwater? "You are, as you know, basically water. Now, when you stare into the liquid around you, there is, in effect, no interface" and as a medium "you have collapsed into yourself" (35). What swimming goggles do is reintroduce a pocket of air—the interface—between our eyes and the ocean, so that we can see clearly again. The seawater even provides a little extra magnification, which is why if you're slightly nearsighted, wearing goggles gives your focus a boost.

global coral reef assessment."[7] NeMO-NET then "leverages NASA's Supercomputer, Pleiades, to use game data to classify and assess the health of coral reefs around the world."[8] Here, the algorithm is interpellated as a student, trained to make more accurate coralations between photographic objects and species and thus assist in establishing baseline estimates of coral populations around the world. Importantly, this process of training the algorithm to make coralations *requires* the labor of humans. They teach the algorithm how to identify corals through tracing them in images; then, scientists to program the app to teach citizen scientists how to accurately identify the corals. Human labor and machine labor co-participate in a cycle of taxonomic accounting, coralating photographic images with coral species.[9] The process of training the algorithm to make accurate coralations is a project of optimization—increasing the speed of image processing and ensuring that such processing is accurate.

Sometimes Coral is not just the subject of optimization, but the model. For example, Google Coral advertises itself as a "complete toolkit to build things with local AI," offering a variety of services: object detection, pose estimation, image segmentation, and key phrase detection.[10] Its logo evokes both the shape of a branching coral and a circuit board, with a circle at the end of each growth tip, in a color that—not surprisingly—is just a touch more orange than PANTONE 16–1546: Living Coral. And like Pantone, Google Coral is selective about its similarities to living corals: it imagines itself as an optimistic, buoyant, even utopian

---

7. NeMO-NET, http://nemonet.info/.

8. NeMO-NET.

9. Unfortunately, when I downloaded NeMO-NET in 2023, most of the photographs had already been classified; no 3D images were left, only low-resolution 2D photographs.

10. Google Coral, https://coral.ai/.

tool for smart cities, and efficient manufacturing, transportation, healthcare, and agriculture. Google's metaphorical invocation of coral does not allude to coral mortality events, bleaching, or climate change; one might imagine degraded data servers, or vulnerable infrastructures. When AI is coral-like, it is about building networks and optimizing the speed and efficiency of business at the local level, not about environmental precarity.[11]

If Great Britain saw coral as a model for empire in the eighteenth and nineteenth centuries, as Elias writes, in the twenty-first-century computer programmers see in Coral a model for optimization problems.[12] Consider programmer Sancho Salcedo-Sanz's particular sense of Coral in a 2014 paper entitled, "The Coral Reefs Optimization Algorithm: A Novel Metaheuristic for Efficiently Solving Optimization Problems." Here, the coral reef optimization (CRO) algorithm is not about making predictions about corals reefs; rather, it uses a selective understanding of coral reef biology as a bio-inspired model, where each coral represents a solution to a problem, encoded as strings of numbers. Each coral/solution is assigned to a square on a grid. The corals then fight for space, and "the reef will progress as long as healthier (stronger) corals (which represent better solutions to

11. Some science-fictional imaginations of corals and AI are not so focused on optimization. Cory Doctorow's short story "I, Row-boat" (2007) imagines a coral reef that suddenly was uplifted into consciousness, in an analogous manner to the AI protagonist of the story: Robbie the row-boat (an obvious pun on robot). The coral reef emerges furious, concerned about its sovereignty and abuse by humans—which could have been admirable in a decolonial context, but is hard to take seriously when its point of view is heavily anthropomorphized. For example, it uses "I/me" pronouns instead of "we/us" (arguably more appropriate for the collective *Umwelt* of coral) and at one point expresses crass enthusiasm for heteronormative sexual relations when it jumps into a human body.

12. Elias, *Coral Empire.*

the problem at hand) survive, while less healthy corals perish."[13] The algorithm also simulates modes of Coral reproduction, specifically: broadcast spawning, brooding, larvae setting, asexual reproduction, and depredation. "This fight for space, along with the specific characteristics of the corals' reproduction, produces a robust metaheuristic algorithm shown to be powerful for solving hard optimization problems."[14] I capitalize Coral in this paragraph to emphasize how little it matters, in the algorithm, *which coral* is modeled; the algorithm relies on precisely the kind of generic and metonymic Coral that I have been keen to critique throughout this book. For Salcedo-Sanz, this universal Coral is useful as a model for solving *other* mathematical optimization problems, such as the "optimum mobile network deployment and off-shore wind farm design."[15]

I see it as a problem that Salcedo-Sanz's model actively ignores key biological and ecological aspects of coral lifeworlds. For example, he abstracts coral into a few basic criteria: taking up space, competing for space, and reproducing. He also conflates algorithmic process with the language of evolution and genetics. In particular, the model replicates a Spencerian version of Darwinian evolution focusing on "survival of the fittest" encoded into a mathematical process. This anachronistic notion of Darwinian evolution ignores many twentieth-century updates, critiques, and qualifications of competition as the defining feature of evolution—specifically, the way that cooperation and symbiosis have also been key drivers, as in the

13. Sancho Salcedo-Sanz et al., "The Coral Reefs Optimization Algorithm: A Novel Metaheuristic for Efficiently Solving Optimization Problems," https://doi.org/10.1155/2014/739768.

14. Salcedo-Sanz et al.

15. Salcedo-Sanz et al.

transformative work of Lynn Margulis.[16] And as noted earlier, Irus Braverman centers symbiosis as a key element of coralations: "The symbiotic algae-microbes-animal relationship at the core of the corals' precarious existence reveals that, more than a single unified entity, corals are 'coralations'—bundles of constantly changing associations that shape and reshape their ways of being in the world and, therefore, the world itself."[17] Although I discuss how cold-water corals are an exception to algal symbiosis in chapter 3, such cooperative ecological arrangements are still common among many corals. These relationships have no place in Salcedo-Sanz's model, which individualizes both corals and solutions. This is, in part, an effect of what Stefan Helmreich identifies as the "genetic algorithm," a "class of procedure that 'evolves' solutions to problems by generating populations of possible solutions, and then by treating these solutions metaphorically as individuals that can 'mate,' 'mutate' and 'compete' to 'survive' and 'reproduce.'"[18]

The algorithm, here, is a site of profound anthropomorphization and individualization. This individualization is possible because Salcedo-Sanz's model operates without the variable of the ocean as an environment, replete with bacteria, viruses, and other floating microbes. Recent discussions of the organismic "holobiont"—a name that accounts for the host plus many other species living in/around it—includes these cooperative

16. See for example Lynn Margulis, *Symbiotic Planet: A New Look at Evolution* (Boston: Basic Books, 1999) that explains the genesis of her theory of endosymbiosis, which—despite initial resistance—is now a well-accepted aspect of how cellular life evolved.

17. Braverman, "Coralations," 2.

18. Stefan Helmreich, "Recombination, Rationality, Reductionism, and Romantic Reactions: Culture, Computers, and the Genetic Algorithm," *Social Studies of Science* 28, no. 1 (February 1998): 39–40.

partners and how they benefit corals.[19] Though some corals do fight each other for space on reefs, their mutualistic relationships with microorganisms erode the easy sense that a coral is only a competitive individual, rather than a "concretion of cooperative processes."[20]

Where does this leave us? Coral photographs form the *content* of data sets upon which algorithms are trained, but corals have also been invoked as the *forms* or models for optimization algorithms. Put more directly: corals are classified by algorithms, and algorithms are sometimes analogized to corals. This is a process of mutual shaping, or backreading, whereby analogy to corals provides some understanding of algorithmic operations, even as algorithms are developed toward studying corals themselves.

Optimization enters into conversations about coral in other ways. Consider the genetic engineering of corals that are optimized for warmer oceans and more acidified seas, or the aquarist's struggle to achieve the optimal conditions for growing coral inside tanks, or the conservationist's attempt to design artificial underwater structures optimized for grafted corals.[21] In these contexts, optimization is about anticipating the sensitivities of coral in a warming world and intervening at the level of the genome, or adjusting the conditions of an artificial environment. Alexander Galloway writes that optimization is highly pragmatic, concerned with the here and now: "[t]he highest point of a curve,

19. Scott F. Gilbert, "Holobiont by Birth: Multilineage Individuals as the Concretion of Cooperative Processes," in *Arts for Living on a Damaged Planet*, ed. Anna Tsing, Heather Swanson, Elaine Gan, and Nils Bubandt, M73–M89 (Minneapolis: Minnesota Pres, 2017).

20. Gilbert, M73.

21. For example, Archireef in Hong Kong, https://archireef.co/; or the USGS suggestion to focus on elkhorn coral, https://www.usgs.gov/programs/cmhrp/news/a-window-opportunity-build-coastal-resilience-how-optimize-coral-restoration.

or alternately the lowest point, the fastest time, or the slowest, the brightest white, the dimmest black, or the greyest grey—the particular quality is unimportant, only the fact that each quality is the 'best,' or at least best suited to the conditions at hand."[22] Coral conservation makes do with un-ideal circumstances in order to optimize coral survivability, but can corals themselves interrupt processes of optimization?

Ken Liu's science fiction short story, "Dispatches from the Cradle: 48 Hours on the Sea of Massachusetts" (2016) explores this very question.[23] "Dispatches" imagines a post-diluvian future where much of Earth's affluent population has fled off-world, leaving behind a far hotter and storm-ravaged Earth for those who could not afford to leave. The people who stayed lead either underground or archipelagic lives. They shelter from the inhospitable Earth through climate-controlled architectures, such as bubbles that can submerge to ride out the worst storms. The story takes the form of a feature article, told by an unnamed journalist who incorporates fragments of writings by a Thoreau-like figure: Asa-<whale>-<tongue>-π (a name incorporating Unicode characters), a former managing director with JP Morgan Credit Suisse on Valentina Station, Venus. Asa "was responsible for United Planet's public offering thirty years ago, at the time the biggest single pooling of resources by any individual or corporate entity in history" and for convincing "a wearied humanity scattered across three planets, a moon, and a dozen asteroid habitats to continue to invest in the Grand Task—the terraforming of both

22. Alexander Galloway, "Perfection – Optimization – Absolution," in *Informatics of Domination,* eds. Zach Blas, Melody Jue, and Jennifer Rhee (Durham, N.C.: Duke University Press, forthcoming 2025).

23. Ken Liu, "Dispatches from the Cradle: 48 Hours on the Sea of Massachusetts," *Lightspeed Magazine* 130 (March 2016), https://www.lightspeedmagazine.com/fiction/dispatches-from-the-cradle-the-hermit-forty-eight-hours-in-the-sea-of-massachusetts/.

Earth and Mars."[24] Asa is introduced as a figure of optimization, a skilled negotiator enacting a vision to return Earth to an optimally habitable climate. Yet she becomes the subject of fascination when, one day, she quits her job as the youngest managing director of JPMCS, divorces her husbands and wives, liquidates her assets, and returns to live on Earth—buying a standard "survival habitat kit, one identical to the millions used by refugee communities all over the planet," and "setting herself afloat like a piece of driftwood."[25] Whereas many science fiction stories ask the question "is it ethical to terraform X planet," "Dispatches" asks: how ethical is it to want to terraform Earth *back* into its previous temperate state, after climate change? For whom might Earth's hotter climate be, in fact, optimal?

This question of optimal climate comes to concern corals and coral-like communities. In one scene, Asa takes the journalist to a notable colony of corals growing in the "Sea of Massachusetts," covering over what was the campus of Harvard University.

Slowly, we descended toward the coral reef that had grown around the ruined hulk of what had once been the largest university library in the world. Around us, schools of brightly colored fish wove through shafts of sunlight, and tourists gracefully floated down like mermaids, streams of bubbles trailing behind their artificial gills. Asa guided the habitat in a gentle circle around the kaleidoscopic sea floor in front of the underwater edifice, pointing out various features. The mound covered by the intricate crimson folds of a coral colony that pleated and swirled like the voluminous dress of a classical flamenco dancers had once been a lecture hall named after Thoreau's mentor, Emerson [. . .] the tiny bump in the side of another long reef, a massive brain-shaped coral formation whose gyri and lobes evoked the wisdom of generations of robed scholars who had once strolled through this hallowed temple of knowledge.

24. Liu.
25. Liu.

Consider how this passage dramatizes a Shakespearean "sea change" not of bones turned into corals, as in Ariel's song in *The Tempest,* but of Harvard's *Widener Library* turned into a *coral reef.* Such a transformation centers the media form of the book, superseded by corals as a surviving informatic form. The corals also evoke another archival form of memory: the human brain. The "intricate crimson folds" of a "massive brain-shaped coral" echo Harvard's school color, and replace a hall named after Emerson. This invocation of brain coral differs from the juxtaposition we saw in Nadia Huggins's photography, in which coral is more like a cognitive extension than a replacement for the "wisdom of generations of scholars."

The reef in "Dispatches" embodies a type of specialized knowledge that is particular to the newly evolved corals: knowledge of how to thrive in the conditions of what Bill McKibben would call *Eaarth,* our planet made alien and unrecognizable due to the intensifications of climate change.[26] In *Adrift,* her memoir within Liu's story, Asa recalls how the corals had unexpectedly, *"developed new symbiotic relationships with artificial nanoplate-secreting algae engineered by humans for ocean-mining"* (italics original) and even acquired their pigments—even Harvard crimson—from heavy metals and pollutants left on Earth. At Widener Library, the corals are particularly bright "because this area was touched by the hand of mankind the longest. Beautiful as they are, these corals are incredibly fragile. A global cooling by more than a degree or two would kill them. They survived climate change once by a miracle. Can they do it again?"[27] For Asa, corals interrupt the fantasy of re-terraforming Earth for

26. Bill McKibben, *Eaarth: Making a Life on a Tough New Planet* (New York: St. Martin's Griffin, 2011).
27. Liu, "Dispatches from the Cradle."

which she had once fought. In this quote, she asks the journalist (narrator) to consider what forms of life would suffer or perish from the re-optimization of the climate for human comfort. Such a question about the *difference* between optimal climates for the new corals and humans engages what media scholar Yuriko Furuhata calls "thermostatic desire," defined as "a technophilic desire to posit atmosphere itself as an object of calibration, control, and engineering."[28] In "Dispatches," the ocean is a space that has become a refuge for corals as well as some human communities, yet the thermostatic desire of re-terraforming could kill off the corals or push out the surviving human communities with re-colonization by off-worlders.

Through Asa's writings, Liu portrays surviving human communities on Earth in a manner similar to the corals (or to use Asa's term, algal mats)—surviving collectives that take refuge underwater. Rather than floating individualistically like the libertarian Seasteading movement, in her memoir, Asa describes communities that are materially interconnected:[29]

> *The floating family habitats connect to each other in tight clan-strands that weave together into a massive raft-city. From above, the city looks like an algal mat composed of metal and plastic, studded with glistening pearls, dewdrops or air bubbles—the transport domes and solar collectors for the habitats. The Singapore Refugee Collective is so extensive that it is possible to walk the hundreds of kilometers from the site of sunken Kuala Lumpur to the surviving isles of Sumatra without ever touching water—though you would never want to do such a thing, as the air outside is far too hot for human survival. When typhoons—a near constant presence at these*

28. Yuriko Furuhata, *Climatic Media: Transpacific Experiments in Atmospheric Control* (Durham, N.C.: Duke University Press, 2022), 2.

29. I offer a critique of Seasteading in "Floating Architectures: Fantasies of Safety in Oceanic Riskscapes," in *Media & Risk*, ed. Bishnupriya Ghosh and Bhaskar Sarkar, 315–27 (New York: Routledge, 2019).

latitudes—approach, entire clan-strands detach and sink beneath
the waves to ride out the storm. The refugees sometimes speak not
of days or nights, but of upside and downside.[30]

Here, the clan-strands are a biotechnical hybrid, evoking marine forms (algal mat, pearls, dewdrops) and anthropogenic materials (metal and plastic). Like the corals that replace Widener Library, the clan-strands come to replace *islands themselves,* an archipelagic substitute connecting "sunken Kuala Lumpur to the surviving isles of Sumatra." Importantly, the movement of submerging is not only associated with loss of cities like Kuala Lumpur and other Atlantis-type figures, but as a strategy of adaptation—a way for the clan-strands to temporarily shelter from atmospheric storms. The capacity for clan-strand habitats to submerge themselves models a new orientation to time, experienced not through "days or nights, but of upside and downside." More than a force of terrestrial dispossession through rising sea levels, the ocean is recoded here as a space of insulation and refuge.

Asa is both the focus of "Dispatches" and but one part of its perspectival constellation. The journalist narrator describes Asa's habitat as appearing like "the pupil of some sea monster's eye staring into the sky" with Asa standing atop, "her back as straight as the gnomon [needle] of a sundial."[31] When the journalist first meets Asa, she "turned and gestured for me to descend through the transparent and open 'pupil' into the most influential refugee bubble in the Solar System."[32] Playing on the pun between pupil-as-student and pupil as an anatomical part of the eye, Asa is a *focalizing* element of the story, and we find Earth's new corals refracted through her perspective. At the same time,

30. Liu, "Dispatches from the Cradle."
31. Liu.
32. Liu.

"Dispatches" challenges Asa's romanticized description of the ocean and Singapore Refugee Collective through the voices of characters who live there: one person who adamantly claims not to be a refugee because they stayed, and one who left for a scholarship off-world but wants Earth to be re-terraformed in order to lessen the suffering of her community. Liu constellates Asa's perspective with these other points of view that question the conditions of sovereignty: who has or should have the power to decide Earth's climate future?

Even if eyes are constant, faces in the story are ever-changing. Upon first meeting Asa, the journalist narrator notes, "she looked exactly like her last public scan-gram" to which she replies, "I don't get many visitors [. . .] There's not much point to putting on a new face every day." This detail suggests a that the technology exists to change one's face as easily as changing clothes. Compare this with Asa's reflections in *Adrift,* where she observes the night sky and proclaims, *"I realized, with a startled understanding reminiscent of the clarity of childhood, that the face of the heavens was a collage,"* with light from each star a different age when it arrives at Earth. Later, Asa writes that *"the surface of the planet is as inconstant as our faces: lands burst forth from the waters and return beneath them; well-armored lobsters scuttle over seafloors that but a geologic eyeblink ago had been fought over by armies of wooly mammoths; yesterday's Doggerland may be tomorrow's Sea of Massachusetts."*[33] Asa appears to naturalize the changeability of the human face through analogy with the collage-like, or mosaic-like, temporality of the face of the heavens; and in so doing, naturalize the surface of the planet as an ever-changing face, suggested by the "geologic

33. Liu.

eyeblink."[34] Such a perspective of constant change might seem to justify the very re-terraforming process that Asa opposes.

Yet in the story, corals are also agents of change, ocean terra-formers and builders that ontologically *are* environments and *make* environments. As environments and builders, then, are coral reefs also a collage that is inconstant? Is the collage an aesthetic form that gives face to otherwise faceless marine in-vertebrates—a form of collectivity that resists optimization?

34. I suggest these art forms interchangeably here; while collages have overlapping pieces and mosaics are traditionally made of nonover-lapping tiles, either could adequately serve as an analogy for the points of starlight that Asa describes.

Conclusion: Edges

IN "A Sonnet at the Edge of a Reef," Chamorro poet Craig Santos Perez introduces a scene full of wonder at the Waikiki Aquarium in Honolulu, Hawaiʻi. As parents take their daughter to a touch tank, "We dip our hands into the outdoor reef exhibit / and touch sea cucumber and red urchin," he writes. Thus begins an intergenerational story of coral reproduction, a "galaxy of gametes / which dances to the surface, fertilizes, opens / forms larvae, roots to the seafloor, and grows, generation / upon generation." The corals take on mythic proportions through analogies: the ocean as galaxy, and gametes as stars. This larger-than-life story could be the content of the next scene where the parents read a children's book, "*The Great Barrier Reef,* to our daughter / snuggling between us in bed." While the daughter is protected, centered between parents, the coral gametes are not. Perez ends his sonnet with the gutting volta: "We don't mention / corals bleaching, reared in labs, or frozen. / And isn't our silence too, a kind of shelter?" This turn introduces an instance of dramatic irony: the parents and/as the reader know of coral bleaching and endangerment, while the child does not.

This scene hits personally for me, since *Coralations* was drafted while I was pregnant with my daughter, to whom this book is dedicated. During this time of expectation, she was gifted a number of ocean-themed children's books by friends and family (Figure 6). Many of these books center tactile elements, like pokable bubble-dots to practice counting, or textured flaps to peek behind. Some portray marine creatures with person-hood, and all introduce a sense of wonder. These books, like the touch tank, stage moments of reciprocity where what is touched also touches back. Such pleasurable moments in books, and at touch tanks, evoke what Eva Hayward poetically calls "fingeryeyes," or the "tentacular visuality of cross-species en-counters" and "synaesthetic quality of materialized sensation."[1] And as Susan G. Davis has written, touch has been central to the way that aquariums market themselves in advertisements, bringing the distance of the ocean and its creatures close at hand, to be felt, to have contact.[2] In the chapter on "Softness" I argued that not all corals are book-like, yet the medium of the book—specifically the children's book—is significant in Perez's poem. The children's book appears as an object in the sonnet, but the sonnet itself is, tonally, a lot like a children's book. The first twelve lines gently explain coral reproduction in a visually enchanting way that would be appropriate for any aquarium docent. To think with Hayward and Licona prepositionally, the form of the children's book is both in and of the sonnet.

The children's book also acts as a type of ecological fetish object, which I use in the anthropological sense of an object that protects against harm. For the parent who knows better, the book uses reassuring educational content to cover over knowledge of

1. Eva Hayward, "FINGERYEYES: Impression of Cup Corals," *Cultural Anthropology* 25, no. 4 (2010): 580.

2. Susan G. Davis, "Touch the Magic," in *Uncommon Ground: Rethinking the Human Place in Nature,* ed. William Cronon, 204–17 (New York: Norton, 1995).

Figure 6. Aurelia reads about reefs. Photograph by Ben Robbins, 2023.

impending species extinctions, climate change, deadly ocean pollution, and—as Perez's poem mentions—coral bleaching. What
underlies the poem's lyrical lullaby is an acute awareness of
coral mortality. Like the daughter listening to a bedtime story
and reflecting on a nice day at the aquarium, perhaps the reader,
too, is lulled to sleep in the first twelve lines of the poem—until
being shaken out of a state of wonder and into raw wakefulness
of ecological mortality. The imagination of the coral bed, and
bedtime story, is a refuge from knowledge of climate change and
forecasts of coral death.

This awareness of coral morality is directly tied to techno-scientific interventions that mediate coral reproduction, mediations that have to do with temperature and temporality. As I wrote in chapters 2 and 3 on "Softness" and "Coldness," thermal imaginaries are central to understanding the iconicity of Coral. Consider the contrast between how Perez describes corals as "reared in labs, or frozen" and a moment earlier in the sonnet, recounted by a docent at the aquarium: "once a year, after the full moon, when tides swell / to a certain height, and saltwater reaches the perfect / temperature, only then will the ocean cue coral / polyps to spawn, in synchrony." In both moments, temperature correlates with different modes of time. The docent's narration of coral reproduction emphasizes ecological process, and the particularity of conditions that have to be met for the magic of coral spawning to occur. Moon, tides, and temperature all combine to alliteratively "cue coral" to "spawn, in synchrony"—synchrony being the word that is spatially placed in the exact center of the sonnet. Synchrony, the doing of things together, connects with the use of "we" in the poem—the "we" that gathers adults and children at the scene of the aquarium and the bedtime story. However, synchrony is also contingent on particular ecological conditions being met—"only then" will the ocean, almost as a musical conductor, "cue coral / polyps to spawn." We might think of this ecological synchronicity as a type of optimization, when "the perfect / temperature" being reached. In chapter 3, the hyperbolic crochet coral reef also entailed an element of synchronicity in producing corals from the labor of many local crafters, their wooly creations timed to the event of exhibition.

By contrast, the corals "reared in labs, or frozen" suggest coldness as a moment of unnatural stasis—embryos frozen in time, for later use, taken out of the lively flow of seawater and into the artificial space of refrigeration. In this frozen storage, they are un-coralated from the rhythms of seasonal spawning. Even though such refrigeration might be well-intentioned by coral conservationists—part of a last-ditch strategy to increase or at least preserve coral populations—refrigeration is a technology with a long history in Pacific contexts that is directly tied to settler colonialism. As Hiʻilei Hobart writes in *Cooling the Tropics: Ice, Indigeneity, and Hawaiian Refreshment* (2023), technologies like refrigeration and air conditioning have been "part of a larger set of strategies employed by settlers to calibrate thermal environments to the aims of territorial expansion, resource extraction, and settler habitation," making warm tropical places across the Pacific more comfortable to Western tastes, and providing the preconditions for local dependency on imported foods.[3] Yet in the context of the sonnet, the refrigeration of coral embryos has an implied coralation with heat. "We don't mention / corals bleaching" alludes to extreme ocean warming events as the cause of coral bleaching in the first place (Chapter 2), warming that has been exacerbated by the anthropogenic emissions of carbon dioxide building up in the atmosphere, largely from nations that historically have been the most active colonizers. For coral reefs, the stress from ocean warming and the response of genetic freezing are both caught up within the global effects of settler colonial histories.

"A Sonnet at the Edge of the Reef" leaves us a final question: what are forms of shelter? The last line, "And isn't our silence, too, a kind of shelter?" uses the adverb "too" as an open signifier; nowhere else in the poem does the word "shelter" occur, so the reader is left wondering not only how silence is a kind of shelter, but what other forms of shelter exist in the poem. To

3. Hiʻilei Julia Kaweipuaakahaopulani Hobart, *Cooling the Tropics: Ice, Indigeneity, and Hawaiian Refreshment* (Durham, N.C.: Duke University Press, 2023), 6.

wonder about other forms of shelter might prompt a rereading: perhaps shelter exists in the educational space of the aquarium, in being caught up listening to a story, or for the child, being nestled between parents. The laboratory is also a shelter, preserving frozen coral embryos. Perhaps we (the reader, the parents, the author) are all too aware that such shelter can only ever be temporary. For Perez, the question of shelter is locative: where is one safe and protected? The title of the poem, too, is about location. The sonnet is not *about* a reef, but *at* the edge of the reef—*at* being a preposition that locates and conjoins—a *graft,* if you will (chapter 3).

As chapters in *Coralations* have explored, the edge of the reef is a site of articulation—in the double sense of being conjoined and of being spoken—across varied media forms: sonnets, photographs, books. Games like NeMO-NET are obsessed with defining edges, especially edges for the boundaries of individual coral colonies. Teaching a neural net how to look for significant edges is the entire reason for the game—enlisting the labor of citizen scientists to play at marking them. In Nadia Huggins's photography edges are extendable, open to new and surprising coralations of form. Soft corals expand and contract their edges with the flow of the tides, inflating in response to the lunar movements of seawater. Cold-water corals have their edges sensed remotely with sonar, through a primarily sonic rather than visual regime of surveyal. In chapter 3, I discussed how cold-water corals thrive on the edges of continental shelves, the same places that coincide with petroleum seeps and infrastructures. Yet the edges of coral reefs are also living, and *made*—as in the crochet fabrications of the Helsinki Reef, where crafters looped petroleum-based yarn into fantastical forms.

My hope for *Coralations* is that it refreshes curiosity about particular corals against the homogeneity of Coral, an icon that belies a multiplicity of lifeforms and, by implication, media forms.[4] Un-coralating corals from Coral creates the space for surprise, a mode of defamiliarization that serves as an opening for other connections to emerge. Not all of these connections fall in the binary of utopia/dystopia; the example of *Lophelia pertusa* growing on oil rigs into artificial reefs, for example, prompts us to attend to a new coralation, a new environmental narrative, that links petroculture with corals—different from the all-too-common association and critique of corals with tropics and tourism. Chapter 2 on "Softness" offered another broken coralation, destabilizing the sense of corals as iconic builders and instead emphasizing a sculptural attention to currents and hydroskeletons, as well as unarchivable conditions of mediation. The goal of attending to coralline "ecologies of comparison," to draw on Tim Choy's phrase, is to better address what slips outside media analogies; not all corals are book-like records, not all corals lend themselves to photomediations.[5] As I wrote in *Wild Blue Media,* "a zoological comparative media studies addresses not only differences in media materiality and form but also the species specificity of media under particular environmental conditions."[6] There is not one reified set of "coral media" for scholars to decode; an analysis of the multispecies necessitates a consideration of multimedia.

Corals can introduce moments of hesitation that ask something of us. They can unsettle habits of the sensory, and in so

4. For a history of the term *lifeform,* see Sophia Roosth and Stefan Helmreich, "Lifeforms: A Keyword Entry," *Representations* 112 (Fall 2010): 27–53.

5. Timothy Choy, *Ecologies of Comparison: An Ethnography of Endangerment in Hong Kong* (Durham, N.C.: Duke University Press, 2011).

6. Jue, *Wild Blue Media,* 26.

doing, invite us to engage with reef ecologies beyond the tired refrain that they need to be saved. My hope is that readers will proliferate ways of relating to corals beyond imagining themselves as saviors, and generate new environmental narratives that refresh public attention. This means taking up the ongoing work of tracing and contesting coralations, a project that is ever in motion.

Acknowledgments

Coralations emerged from a series of lectures I wrote for a seminar on "Coral Mediations" at the Summer School for Global Studies and Critical Theory at University of Bologna in July 2022, coorganized with Duke University and the University of Virginia. Thank you to Ranjana Khanna for the invitation to participate, to Antonio Schiavulli for his hospitality, and to the graduate students in the course: Ilaria Bonvicini, Stephen Borunda, Nicolaas Buitendag, Francesco Casales, Michael Cavuto, Mariachiara Ficarelli, Haley Elzsatz, Scott Erich, Archit Guha, Maria Molano, and Caio Santos. My thanks to Stefan Helmrich for sharing feedback on an early draft, to Colin Milburn for a helpful conversation about citizen science games, and to Erik Cordes for sharing expertise on deep-sea corals. I also want to acknowledge the students in my graduate course on "Ocean Mediations" during winter 2023, whose questions and contributions influenced my thought as I was working through the conceptual framing of this book: Nadia Ahmed, Olivia Bievenue, Henry Coburn, Mary Cook, Arushi Gupta, Becca Hamilton, Bridge McWaid, Robin Satori, Saide Singh, Gil Vitro, and Tinghao Zhou. Margaret Cohen brought Stacy Alaimo, Elizabeth Deloughrey, and myself into lively oceanic conversation at Stanford in April 2024, an early window to share the ideas in this book, for which I am grateful.

I also appreciate the opportunity to speak about Coralations at the University of Hawaii, Manoa; the University of Toronto; the University of Richmond; and the EASLCE conference in Perpignan, France. Thank you to my editor at Minnesota Press, Leah Pennywark; copyeditor Michael Stoffel; and to an anonymous reader who contributed thoughtful suggestions on the manuscript.

Coralations is dedicated to my daughter Aurelia, who arrived just after I drafted this book. She is wondrous. I am grateful for the love and companionship of my partner, Ben Robbins, who kindly took the photograph in Figure 6. Thank you to my mom, Terry Jue, for everything—I understand now!—my sister, Lori Jue, and Theo the labrador. I like to think my dad, Rodney Jue, would have enjoyed the soft corals in this book. It truly takes a village: a special note of gratitude to my dear friend Alenda Chang, to my colleagues in the English Department and in Film and Media Studies at UCSB, and to those who checked in on us: Yanoula Athanassakis, Beata Belfield, Zach Blas, Jinita Bhulabhai, E. Cook, Mona Damluji and Jia-ching Chen, Ridhika Dhani, Jeremy Douglass and Holly Rushing, Bishnupriya Ghosh and Bhaskar Sarkar, Baron Haber, Heidi Amin-Hong, Jim Kearney and Emily Zinn, Lauren Pawlak, Mihai Putinar and family, Swati Rana, Daniel Reeve, Jennifer Rhee, Amrah Solomon, Jean Schultz, Kimberlee Uwate, Chris Walker, and many more who celebrated Aurelia's arrival.

(Continued from page iii)

Forerunners: Ideas First

Marquis Bey
The Problem of the Negro as a Problem for Gender

Cristina Beltrán
Cruelty as Citizenship: How Migrant Suffering Sustains White Democracy

Hil Malatino
Trans Care

Sarah Juliet Lauro
Kill the Overseer! The Gamification of Slave Resistance

Alexis L. Boylan, Anna Mae Duane, Michael Gill, and Barbara Gurr
Furious Feminisms: Alternate Routes on *Mad Max: Fury Road*

Ian G. R. Shaw and Marv Waterstone
Wageless Life: A Manifesto for a Future beyond Capitalism

Claudia Milian
LatinX

Aaron Jaffe
Spoiler Alert: A Critical Guide

Don Ihde
Medical Technics

Jonathan Beecher Field
Town Hall Meetings and the Death of Deliberation

Jennifer Gabrys
How to Do Things with Sensors

Naa Oyo A. Kwate
Burgers in Blackface: Anti-Black Restaurants Then and Now

Arne De Boever
Against Aesthetic Exceptionalism

Steve Mentz
Break Up the Anthropocene

John Protevi
Edges of the State

Matthew J. Wolf-Meyer
Theory for the World to Come: Speculative Fiction and Apocalyptic Anthropology

Melody Jue is associate professor of English at the University of California, Santa Barbara. She is author of *Wild Blue Media: Thinking through Seawater* and coeditor of *Saturation: An Elemental Politics.*

N. Adriana Knouf
How Noise Matters to Finance

Andrew Culp
Dark Deleuze

Akira Mizuta Lippit
**Cinema without Reflection: Jacques Derrida's Echopoiesis
and Narcissism Adrift**

Sharon Sliwinski
Mandela's Dark Years: A Political Theory of Dreaming

Grant Farred
Martin Heidegger Saved My Life

Ian Bogost
The Geek's Chihuahua: Living with Apple

Shannon Mattern
Deep Mapping the Media City

Steven Shaviro
No Speed Limit: Three Essays on Accelerationism

Jussi Parikka
The Anthrobscene

Reinhold Martin
Mediators: Aesthetics, Politics, and the City

John Hartigan Jr.
Aesop's Anthropology: A Multispecies Approach